Contents

Acknowledgements

I would like to acknowledge the vast amount of time and effort given by my friend and author, Alan Nixon, and for the patience of his wife and family. My thanks also go to Stephen Lownsbrough and the staff at Nelson & Co for their co-operation. Finally, thanks to everyone who has shared in my memories throughout this book and my life in general.

Foreword
by Walter Smith

I signed Stuart for Rangers and in our years together at Ibrox he typified the success we had. He was a major part of the side and while people will talk about the Ally McCoists and Mark Hateleys and others before him, from a manager – and player – point of view he was appreciated as much as anyone.

Stuart set the tone. His attitude and commitment summed up the side. We were not the most gifted team, but we never lacked heart or that will to win and Stuart had plenty of both and was a great example.

We had nobody better in that respect. He would win the ball for us and had such a big heart. We were a team that never liked getting beaten and he was the main reason for that.

It's a disappointment to me that through injury we didn't get the most out of him in the last couple of years. It was the first time he had been out of the picture with a serious problem.

Stuart was part of that great camaraderie and spirit that was built up between the lads and when a team breaks up that ends too. It will be recreated with the next side, but Stuart feels that after being such a big part of that era it is time for the younger ones to come through.

Although Stuart is a Scot he was brought up in England, yet he took everything about Rangers on board when he signed.

He took on the mentality of the supporters and any of the fans looking at him saw one of them, a player committed to the cause.

I wish him well in the next chapter of his career and I am sure he will give it everything as he always does.

Walter Smith
June 1998

Chapter 1

Happy days

I was born on 10 June 1964, better late than never. You could say I was an unexpected arrival. Mum Jean and dad Andy already had a grown-up family in their home in Leeds – big brother Leslie was 20 before I turned up and sister Janette was coming up for her 16th birthday. Obviously I wasn't planned. Contraception was not such a sure thing in my dad's day, he told me later. It is safe to say I was a wee mistake.

Still I arrived into a football world. Even if my dad Andy had hung up his boots I grew up learning about his exploits. Both my folks came from Hamilton and were proud of it. Dad came south to play football and was one of the Five Ms in the Blackpool side after the Second World War. That's Matthews, Mortensen, McIntosh, Munro and, of course, McCall to those who don't know the history of the Seasiders. Dad moved on to West Brom and then my beloved Leeds where he was in the team with the legendary John Charles and a youngster called Jackie Charlton. Dad was an inside left and good enough to play for Scotland's B team against Northern Ireland.

Not that I needed to go far to get my fix of football. For the first year we lived round the corner from Elland Road. The house was just up the road from the chip shop opposite the ground. Ironically that was the place I was to spend most Saturday afternoons and became the venue of my favourite football memory. We moved out to Wortley, but watching Leeds United was my first taste of the game when I was just six. Dad took me or my sister-in-law Jeanette would go along with me and a little stool to stand on so that I could see over the top of the terraces. I was there when Leeds put seven past Southampton in a game that *Match of the Day* showed over and over again. That is my first recollection of a football crowd. They roared 'Olé' every time the Leeds players put passes together. It was then I realised that football could be a pleasure.

We were a sporty family. My mum and sister played netball and hockey and my brother Leslie, the lucky one of us born in Scotland, and brother-in-law Alan played for Saturday and Sunday league teams locally. It was no surprise that I was keen even at my first primary school, Upper Wortley. At the age of nine I went to Thornhill Middle School and that was when the fun and the trouble started.

We had a cup semi-final against Manston on the Saturday and the night before I fell off a tree. Mum took me to hospital for x-rays. I had severely sprained my wrist and damaged a small bone in my arm. This sergeant-major of a nurse put the arm in a sling, told me under no circumstances to take any physical exercise for two weeks and strictly banned me from playing football. So next morning was the game and the park was just a minute down the road. My mum said: 'No, don't even think about playing.' I told her I would say to the teacher I couldn't play, but she realised I was telling a little porky when she saw my boots were hidden under my good arm in a bag. I tried to pretend I was taking them for a friend who might need them. She left me with the words, 'You've been warned.'

I tried my best to keep my word. However, we had just 11 fit players and no sub. I asked if I could be 12th man, so that at least I would be involved. It was fatal. The teacher let me. The score went to 3-3 and into extra-time. At half-time a boy on the wing went over on his ankle and had to come off. It was my turn. They put me out on the wing, hoping I wouldn't get hurt and I was trying not to look too silly with my arm in a sling.

There was just a minute left when glory came at a corner. The ball landed at my feet on the penalty spot and I put a peach of a volley into the goal. It was Roy of the Rovers stuff, or as I would later learn Coisty of the Rangers stuff. In the celebrations my sling was ripped off. Two hours later I was back in hospital getting a real dressing-down from my dad, my mum and that nurse. If that was not bad enough I also missed the Leeds v Liverpool game that afternoon and they were always crackers. I was grounded for a week. Was it worth it? You bet. Three weeks later we won the final and I got my first-ever trophy. You don't get pleasure without a bit of pain.

Sadly my mum and dad split up when I was 11. Dad worked as a travelling salesman around Britain, just returning at weekends. After the split I stayed with my mum, but still saw dad some weekends. We moved in with my sister Janette and her husband Alan plus their twins Jane and Karen and nephew John. Imagine, I was an uncle at the age of five. After the split I put all my time into sports – maybe it was my way of blocking out what had happened. The teachers at school were great and encouraged me. I was in before classes started to play basketball and badminton and table tennis at lunchtime and athletics afterwards. I think I focused all my attentions on doing sports because of the way things were. I even managed to play for Yorkshire at table tennis, but I lost 11-0 once when I represented them and that was as low as you could get. It was not for me.

Football was always my game. I got into the Leeds under-11 boys team and I was made skipper. We won a county trophy and there were some good players in the side. It was an obsession, a great love. And it also got me the cane for the one and only time in my life. One morning assembly the headmaster told us he was cracking down on bad time-keeping at breaks and warned us of the consequences. As it does, it went in one ear and came out the other by lunchtime. It was the usual 20-a-side at the back of the playground and the score was 9–9, next goal's the winner, and the bell goes. What was a boy to do? Five minutes later it was two-a-side and the local bravehearts were sweating like mad looking for that elusive victory. My wee pal fired the winner between two coats being picked up by . . . the headmaster. It was straight down to his office for six of the best. Sore, but it was worth it. We won 10–9 after all.

Thanks to my 'aunt' Betty Tate I also got the chance to pick up another special award from one of my Leeds United heroes, Eddie Gray. She wrote into the local paper and entered me for a competition to find the most dedicated sports-mad kid in town. She said I played this and that and still had time to watch United. The prize was £25 of gear from the Leeds United club shop and I won. I even got the afternoon off school to go and collect the goodies.

The trophies were coming in on the pitch too. The Leeds City Boys side won the Yorkshire Cup, beating teams like Barnsley and Scunthorpe along the way. We played on Saturday mornings, so I still had time to get down to Elland Road. Apart from the fact they were my local team there were also so many Scots in the side and I obviously identified with Billy Bremner. The red hair, the midfield play, the aggression. But there was also David Harvey in goal, the Gray brothers, Peter Lorimer, Arthur Graham and then later Gordon McQueen and Joe Jordan. For all that, my top man was Tony Currie. I just loved his skill and the way he strolled round the midfield playing passes and just dominating the pitch. Funny that, as I have never managed to reach that level myself, as everyone keeps reminding me. However, I do have proof that there was a bit of the Currie in me. One local paper described a goal I created for Leeds schools at Liverpool as being 'like the type Tony Currie would have been proud of in his prime'. It was too. I went on a mazy dribble, starting with a spin out wide and left a Liverpool defender sprawling before cutting the ball back for a lad called Gary Chapman to slip it home. I don't know what came over me. At that time, because I was so small, the skill had to get me by. The power and the strength were to come later.

I also learned that my football could make up for my lack of height when we moved to one of the toughest areas in Leeds, Wyther Park. At least you could say it toughened me up a bit.

It was a tough housing estate, a rough area that fortunately has just about been knocked down. It was where we were sent by the council and was the only place we could get. We were on the eighth floor of the high-rise flats and above some of the trouble down below. My mum was working all hours to keep us going. She was a secretary and did loads of overtime to kit me out, for which I will always be grateful. Because she wasn't home until late that was another good reason to spend so much time doing sports. I didn't really fancy being home alone around there if I could help it. I went on football trips to places like Spain and Italy and it was only because mum scraped the cash together to afford it. Times were tight and while other kids had the Scalextrix I was more than happy to get boots. When some of the boys in the team had brand new Adidas boots I got mine from Asda. I even had to stuff school exercise books down my socks once because I did not have any shinpads. That did not go down too well the next day when I took these dirty jotters to the classroom.

Don't get the idea I was pushed into being a footballer. I was encouraged, but it was all around me and I enjoyed being part of it. My brother and brother-in-law were keen players and I even went along to their games and cut up the oranges and took down the nets. They played for the Hannover Arms. Alan was a silky, elegant midfielder and Les a hard-tackling, aggressive centre-half. Or so they said. I found out at the games that Alan was known as Ducker Donald because he was frightened to head the ball and Les was put in defence where it was the only chance of being picked in the side (only joking, lads). Because I was a reasonable player it got me out of a lot of scrapes in that company. At the age of 14 I was playing for pub teams among grown men who looked after me. If there was any bother on the estate I knew the names I could mention and people would back off. 'Don't touch him, lads, he's playing for us on Sunday.'

I just loved football and all the banter in the dressing-room after games. I was hooked. It also made me laugh to see these big guys, breathing out of their backsides at the end of games and saying they would have to work on their fitness to improve. An hour later they were down the pub on their fifth pint, fag in hand, saying how much better they felt. And, yes, there were some 'doings' off the park despite my 'mafia' backers. It was probably because I was the new kid on the block and got into a few skirmishes. The fact I could play football helped me out as it got some respect in the area.

On the serious football side I was now playing with Pudsey Juniors, who were the nursery side for Farsley Celtic. In turn they were a big breeding ground for Leeds United. All the local lads who made good came up through those ranks, people like Paul Madeley and Paul Reaney. So that was the place for me to start my bid to play for Leeds too. We had a good lad just older than me called Kevin Broadhurst who joined Birmingham City. It was good to have an example of someone you could see making his way to the top. I also had a great youth boss called Alan Cowley. We used to go all round Yorkshire. We didn't play in a league, we were the Harlem Globetrotters of local football, too good for that. That was where I learned the three As, application, attitude and ability. I never did have a problem with the first two. I started to dream about the big-time at that age. Mr Cowley took us down to Birmingham to see how Broadhurst was doing. It was my first look inside a league club and I was impressed.

By this time I was at Harrington School which was all-male, a bit unfortunate, but at least I could concentrate on my sports. There was no time to be chasing the lassies. Not that I would win any beauty contests after breaking my nose for the first time playing cricket. Me, a Yorkshireman, smacked in the face when I bent down for a ball and it simply jumped up and hit me. They had to stop the game as there was blood everywhere and the umpire had to take me to hospital. The lads were far from happy. We were about to win.

Still, the football team at school was going well. We had one of the best under-15 teams going. However, we had a few layabouts who didn't fancy turning up for training. The teacher got mad and warned them he would drop them for a big final coming up if they didn't show. Two or three of them were really good players, but weren't into football. It was just an enjoyment for them, they wanted to do other things and then turn up for games. The day we met Cardinal Heanon's School in the final they got a shock. The teacher stuck to his guns and left them out. It looked like madness as the opposition had six players who were representing Leeds City for their age and they were odds-on to beat us. The 'stars' who were left out of our team were sneering at us and told us we would get thumped. The boys in the team, in the nicest possible way, were more like rugby league players. They had only just started playing football, but they went out that day and gave their all. We somehow got a 1–1 draw and shared the trophy. I will always remember that day as it taught me about attitude. They wanted to be part of it. You don't have to be the best of players, but you have to have that desire in you. It was also an extra thrill being the underdogs and proving everyone wrong.

I also played for a team called Holbeck, who were the first club I went abroad with. On one trip we spent a day at the Nou Camp stadium in Barcelona. I went on to the middle of the pitch and just took a long look round and wondered what it would be like to play there. I was getting a real taste for it by now. However, there was a problem and for a year or so it looked like being one I could not get over too easily. Simply I was not putting on any weight or growing any taller. For a year I seemed to stand still and it was a major worry. Everyone else in the team was a head bigger than me, they could head the ball better and boot it further. I was being left behind. My dad went to one game and pulled the coach aside to ask him why I was only sub. 'What's the score?' he said. The poor guy said he thought I would make it, but I would have to wait until I was bigger and stronger. Dad asked if he had ever seen a footballer before and reeled off all the great little 'uns like Alan Ball, Johnny Giles and Bobby Collins . . . and himself. I was embarrassed, but the coach never had an answer. Dad had made his point.

For a season I just frittered away my chances. I wasn't playing for the team that was the breeding ground for Leeds United. I could see it all slipping away. I was coming on for a few minutes and getting the odd game, but wasn't figuring in the important matches. I joined Farsley Celtic and out of a squad of 13 nine of them got apprenticeships at league clubs. David Harrison and Tim Hotte went to Arsenal, a couple more were off to Nottingham Forest, four went to Leeds. Bobby Peel even made the first team that way. Another lad went to Manchester United, although I can't recall his name.

I thought I had missed out, all washed up at 15. I started writing to banks and was planning to pass my exams, convinced that my idea of being a footballer had gone. I was the same weight and the same size as a year before and people were overlooking me because of it. Then one day Farsley played Bradford City's Juniors in a friendly. It changed my life for good. Frankly they were not much good at the time and I had a good game. Along with another boy they asked me for a trial. For the first time I was given the chance to show what I could do. The wee man was off the shelf. I did well in my first match and out of courtesy they kept me on for four games. Then it was four games in the reserves at places like Southport. To me it was Wembley.

The man running the Bradford reserve team was Brian Edwards and the boss of the club was George Mulhall. There were old pros like Alan Gilliver, later the club's stadium manager, still playing and it was a great experience. You were going on trips on the bus, playing cards up the back and tucking into chips on the way home, just feeling the part. They also had a hopeful youngster called Mark Ellis who was to become one of my best mates. He was a couple of years older and never had to clean the boots like I did when I was taken on, something he enjoys reminding me of. Those games were like World Cup finals to me. I treated them so seriously while others were maybe just killing time. I didn't think I had done enough in those 'trial' matches, but I obviously had impressed someone. It was still a big surprise when they took me on.

Just two weeks before my exams word came through that I was being given a two-year apprenticeship by Bradford. The revision just went out of the window, I couldn't concentrate.

My mum kept saying to stick at it, but my mind was away. In the end I got two 'O' levels, in English and Modern Geography. But it didn't matter, I was going to be a footballer.

I was asked down to see the manager on the night of Peter Downsborough's testimonial. I went on the train and then the bus with my agent, mum. Straightaway she hit it off with the manager George because they were both Scots. A couple of whiskies later I was signed on the dotted line. A bit of patter later and I was getting £20 a week and digs money (that probably swung it) of another £15 a week. Not to forget the bus pass thrown in. I could not join officially until my 16th birthday but on that day I was in the door.

Away from my new 'living' I regularly went up to Scotland for holidays. The family came from Hamilton and my cousin Billy was Rangers daft. He took me to Ibrox for the first time to see Rangers play Dundee. On the supporters' bus I got the Rangers number nine, big Colin Stein, and he got the Rangers number two, Sandy Jardine, in the sweep for the first goal. We got to the game and stood in the Copeland Road end and immediately Stein barged his way into the box, rounded the keeper . . . and was brought down. I had counted my money before he was tripped. I told Billy he wouldn't get a penny when Stein scored from the spot. I was stunned to find out Jardine took the penalties. Although Leeds were my local team I always had a big place in my heart for Rangers. I could never imagine then that I would get to play for them.

When I was 14 and 15 I used to go and watch Leeds play as often as I could. I was in their supporters' club. I didn't tell mum I was going on some away trips because there was usually bother. Once we went to Derby and there was a big commotion but I never really got too involved.

My dad was a Hamilton Accies fan, but any time we went I never paid. There was a place behind the goal where my cousin Gary and I could sneak in for nothing. If anyone from the club is reading this, don't send a bill, although I must owe them a fortune. We stood behind the goal near their famous fan, Fergie. He gave me a football education in abusing players, from your team and theirs. He always gave me

Featuring.......STUART McCALL

Stuart played for Thornhill Middle School in his first year at the age of nine, and towards the end of that season he played for the Leeds' Schools under 11 team. He was a regular in that team the following season when they won the Yorkshire Trophy, and also helped his school team to become joint winners of the Samuel Cup as the champions of Leeds.

Stuart made tremendous progress last season. He is now a skilful player with an astonishing work rate and an attitude which has changed completely. If he keeps developing in the same way, he must stand a good chance of joining the long list of our boys who have made their way into the professional game.

His favourite team is Glasgow Rangers and his favourite player Tony Currie.

. . . .

Our thanks to Jim Armfield for the quote for our first programme this season. As the manager of Yorkshire's only First Division club, we are pleased that he is the first personality to honour us with his signature. We wish Jim and Leeds United the best of good fortune for the future.

. . . .

I wish Pudsey Juniors every success, and at the same time would like to tell you that if you are going to reach the top, then nothing less than total dedication will get you there. You will never get more out of the game than you put in. Good luck to you all.

Jim Armfield

Testimony, from a more than respectable English source, of my early allegiance to the Rangers cause pelters when I played them. Accies had some cracking players at the time in Phil Bonnyman and Neil Hood. They even beat Leeds 4-3 one night in a pre-season friendly and I was one of those in a packed ground to enjoy it. No wonder I would go back to school after the holidays with a Scottish accent when I mixed with my lot up there.

Visiting Scotland was special but I also spent some happy holidays with Janette, Alan and the kids at their caravan in Sewerby near Bridlington. Mum was working and I got sent up for a few days. Dad took me to Rothesay too when I was 11 – it was my first time on a ferry. He showed me all the islands on the way over and I have sharp memories of that.

Times were tough but maybe it's better that way as life can be too easy when you're given everything. You appreciate things more when you have to work for them. That's helped me in life as well as in football. You get back what you put in. I've tried to keep my values and a lot of that dates back to the days when I was getting by as a kid. I look back at my childhood, and even though my parents split up, they were good days. It could have been a sad time, but it wasn't.

Chapter 2

Can I have a
long weight, please?

I made my mark on Bradford City pretty quickly as an apprentice. Well, I put the 'Welcome to Valley Parade' sign up on the outside of the ground as one of my jobs. It was a hard working day, starting early and doing all the run-around stuff. There were only three of us at the time because that's all the club could afford. John Hanson and Carl Leneghan were the other two. We were groundsmen – I had to put the divots back at the end of games – painters of the crush barriers, cleaners of the bath, it was your life. I was also the boot boy and had 32 pairs to do, shining them up and even making the soles gleam for the players I liked who looked after me. The youngsters today don't know they are born. Scrubbing floors and pulling the hairs out of the bath, they don't realise what life was like in those days for a young hopeful like me.

Obviously I was keen to impress, so on the first day Brian Edwards asked me to go to the chemist and get him a couple of plasters. Before I went I heard this hoarse Irish voice behind me. I had been told about this guy and to look out when he was about. It was Bobby Campbell. I thought I would impress him and told him I was going up to the chemist, so did he want some lozenges for his throat? In two seconds he had me up against the wall by the throat with my legs dangling and let me know in his own style that he always talked like that. Here was me trying to be a nice boy and a credit to the community and that was my reward. I was trembling for hours after. Bobby was not a man to cross. Mind you he did let me get him some Anadin for his hangover when I was at the shops.

I didn't have an option when I joined Bradford, but that was good luck. They were a Fourth Division side who had just missed out on promotion. If I had been picked up by Leeds with all their players and history I would have been the one starting at the bottom, but Bradford gave me my big chance and I was determined to repay them. Of all my pals at Leeds City who went to big clubs only two turned pro and they were out of the game a couple of years later. I was starting at the bottom with only one way to go.

Although the jobs were difficult as an apprentice I was thrown in with the first-team players to train. I mixed with good pros with good habits and great crack and I was eager to learn from them. People like David McNiven and Mick Bates had played at a higher level with Leeds, while Terry Dolan had been at Arsenal. Bobby Campbell was the main man. Other guys like Ces Podd, Les Chapman and Gary Watson were really helpful. I was their slave from the start of the day to the finish. If anything wasn't right, like a pair of socks missing, I would get it in the neck. We had a Scottish coach, Lammie Robertson, who was good to me. We shared the same passion for Scotland and he looked out for me.

But even your friends like a wind-up and I fell for one famously. Lammie told me that Brian Edwards wanted me to go out in my lunch hour to Madeley's DIY store down the hill and ask the manager for a 'long weight' he needed for some work he was doing on the gym. Now normally I would also get the pies during lunch and bring them back for the rest of the lads, but like a good apprentice I went into the store first and said I had been sent down for a 'long weight' and could they give me one. The boy on the check-out went into the back office and another assistant came. 'Are you from Bradford City? Oh, you're the one who wants the long weight. We'll give you one all right.' Half-an-hour passed and no one came out, I was panicking because I thought the boys would be missing their lunch because of me. An hour was nearly up when the assistant came out again. 'There you are,' he said. 'You've had a really long wait now.' It dawned on me. I felt two inches tall and my face went bright red. I got back to the ground and they were all waiting for me. I said: 'You don't really think I fell for that one? Anyway, here are your pies . . . and they're cold.' I've used that line a couple of times since myself. It was good craic.

It was certainly not two years wasted. You did some crap jobs, but you were always playing. I was up early to catch two buses to the ground, but I felt I was getting somewhere. The carrot at the end of it was worth waiting for. When big John Hanson turned pro it left just two of us and that was nearly impossible. Bradford were so hard-up at the time. They took on a couple of apprentices a year while Leeds would have 12, although you would be shocked if one or two made it from that amount. If Bradford got one pro out of theirs they would be delighted.

Those reserve games were special to me. I used to do my own reports on them, give myself marks out of ten. I was playing on Valley Parade and going to big grounds against old pros like Norman Hunter. It was some experience. I must have looked out of place because at 16 I still looked like I was 12. I was just eight stones. They tried to build me up with vitamins, iron tablets and glucose drinks. The club also told me to eat steaks, which was a shock to mum for it was another big expense. In the first six months at Bradford I put over a stone on and that helped.

My debut came at just 16 in a testimonial for Ces Podd on 30 March 1981. It was the first black player's testimonial and he had an all-black select with some top players like Cyrille Regis and the Fashanu brothers. I was still doing my duties before the game and sorted out the players with shorts, but could only find an oversize pair for myself. They were bigger than my body. The crowd roared when I came on – with laughter. There was this little kid with shorts blowing in the wind. I remember going down the wing and they were flapping about. It must have been hilarious to see me out there against guys almost twice my size. I hope Ces did well out of the night because he was great, he gave me lifts home when he could although not always like the one I got that night. His car was full and I had to jump in the back . . . and sat on Tessa Sanderson's knee. She was a big sporting celebrity at the time and had come up to the game. That was my claim to fame and I have witnesses. When I squeezed out of Ces's car a mate was waiting outside the chippie for me and couldn't believe his eyes.

It wasn't all glamour like that. The reserves were in the North Midlands League, but I was making progress and was named captain at just 16. My dad came down one night without telling me to watch a game. He thought I was taking too much on being skipper as well and wrote me a letter explaining why I should drop that job. Somebody must have been noticing because I was picked for an FA Colts XI against a Young England side that November, a big honour for a Bradford player. David Seaman was the goalkeeper, but the only thing I can recall of the day was what stuffed shirts ran the team. 'Don't get your strips dirty,' one said. You what? I went with high expectations and came away thinking about their stiff upper lips.

I was in the first-team squad for the 1980–81 season, mainly because we were not going to go up or down. I was there for the experience and to carry the hampers. We never stayed overnight before away games because the club could not afford it. But you were on the bus, wearing the blazer and feeling like a player. I must admit my heart was still with Leeds United and any away trips that were too far I would stay back and watch them on Saturdays. I had a great scam going with my pal Paul Duckworth. My dad would get us two tickets put on the gate, we would ask David McNiven to have two left for free too, but in another name. We got there early, picked them up and then sold them off at face value. Four tickets at three quid each left us with enough to get in the terraces for £1.50 each. You could have a good Saturday night out with nine quid between you in those days. We were living off Leeds United for a couple of years and they never knew.

One of my best memories of that first season at Bradford was when Liverpool came to Valley Parade for a Milk Cup tie. I remember helping Bob Paisley and Joe Fagan put their skips back on the team bus after the game. It was a relief to these two older gents that I could lift the heavy weights up the stairs to the bus. When they said thanks Mr Paisley slipped a tenner into my hand as a tip. I could hardly catch my breath – that was half a week's wages just for doing a small job. I managed to sneak Graeme Souness's tie-ups back in the dressing-room too. What a night. We even won the game 1-0 and I had picked up an illegal payment!

I was sad when George Mulhall left and disappointed that Lammie went too. To be fair Roy McFarland came in and gave the place a buzz. He was a former England player and a top name. He also brought in someone who would be a huge influence on me in Mick Jones, his assistant. Although I had done well the previous season I was now back in the reserves and never played during that 1981–82 season. McFarland was going for promotion, concentrating on that and leaving Mick Jones with lads like me. His philosophy was that if you give your best that was all that mattered. You don't have to be great. He just asked that I listened to him and he helped me develop into a player.

By that time I had filled out quite a bit and even grown a few inches. I was going away with the team sometimes, but just to keep me in touch. Of course I was still watching Leeds, but combining the two was tricky. One time I made the sub's bench for the last game at Mansfield, then played right back in an end-of-season challenge against Sheffield United when we had both won promotion. Ces missed the game with an eye injury and I filled in at right-back. I got a knock on the ankle and it had to be strapped up, but I wasn't going to miss the next big game . . . watching Leeds fight against relegation at West Brom. I went down with Paul, but it was a nightmare. We lost and the fans trashed the ground at the end of the match. The atmosphere was bad going home on the bus and my ankle was giving me some pain because I had been standing on it all night. We took a taxi home and the driver spent the ten minutes telling us he was pleased Leeds had gone down and what scum Leeds fans were, not knowing we were two of them. I looked at my mate and said: 'We're not having this.' I told the driver to stop about half a mile from the house and we jumped out without paying and legged it. I forgot about my bad ankle and was hobbling along – the old driver nearly caught me but I knew the back lanes and escaped. That will teach him, I thought. I hope he didn't miss the four quid, but maybe he will know not to go on so much next time he has a Leeds fan in the back.

That summer of 1982 I was given a year's contract as a professional. No matter how well you think you are doing you are never sure until your name goes on that form. It was the end of all the dirty jobs. I don't know if McFarland ever fancied me, but I know Mick Jones was keen. My contract was £50 a week and up to £20 for an appearance.

The start of the next season flew round and I got my chance while Ces was out having an operation on his eye. I made my debut against Reading at right-back and I did okay. The papers thought I was the best player and Mick Jones was very complimentary. It was our first match in the Third Division and I stayed in for four games. McFarland pulled me out and said it was for my own good. I was in and out for a while before McFarland left for Derby and caused a storm. He was branded a Judas and no one could understand why he went to a club in the same division after building such firm foundations at Bradford. I believe he was right because he had so many older players at Bradford, he probably thought they could not go much further. Apart from me, Peter Jackson and Mark Ellis the team was getting on. When McFarland left we lost a player as well as a manager, but I was more upset about Mick going. I took a lot from him in general and just when I was making progress he was off.

The timing was strange because we were playing Manchester United in the Milk Cup. Brian Edwards was caretaker and we drew the first leg. I came in for the second in midfield. We lost 4–1 and were down early. United were flying with people like Bryan Robson and Remi Moses in the team. We took a big support and it was brilliant when we scored a goal for them. To play on that surface and in front of that crowd gave me a real taste. The game went by in a flash but I do remember one United youngster coming on with the fans singing his name, Norman Whiteside. I found out about him soon enough when I went to pick the ball up as it went out of play. He came right through me and sent me on to the track. Thanks, Norman, that's when I discovered I needed a bit more building up.

I was finding out about football life that season. A trip to Bournemouth always sticks in my mind. We went on the Friday night and it was foggy. The boss let us go out for a stroll and big Bobby Campbell reckoned the game would be off for sure. So he took us for a pint or two, although I was only on orange juice. Next day the fog was still thick but the ref could see both goals from the centre circle so the match went on. Bournemouth had a big centre-half with no teeth called John Impey who didn't take to me. I stood behind the keeper at one stage and kicked the ball out of his hands as he tried to clear. I put the ball in the net and the ref gave a goal as he couldn't see what had happened with all the fog. My first 'goal' in senior football, or so I thought. The linesman, who couldn't have seen much either, was flagging away. As I went back to the centre circle I felt this hand take me by the throat. It was Impey and he wanted to discuss the 'goal'. Next second my minder Bobby was there from out of the mist and he and Impey were going at it. A riot over me. Bobby gave me a real roasting afterwards, for Impey had been going down his ankles every time from then on. All that and a hangover, poor old Bob.

I was learning to handle myself and was capable of the odd prank as well. A few of us went to college in Leeds with some of the United boys and once we went on an Outward Bound break. We had a competition between the Bradford and Leeds boys and won the relay race. The verbals were going. That night we sneaked into their rooms and put a mattress out of the window. The weather turned and the rain came down, soaking the mattress. The Leeds coach, a guy called Keith Mincher, gave us all a lecture on how stupid we Bradford boys had been. He gave me some stick in particular. 'I don't suppose you do anything like that at your club,' he sneered. Little did he know that when I told them they were delighted. But then he said: 'Maybe that's why Leeds are in the First Division and Bradford in the Third.' When I look back maybe that is why Leeds were on the way down. They had players from all over while we were knit together tightly at Bradford. Mincher's comments hurt, but in the end I had the last laugh. Bradford were on the up, Leeds started to fall and he was sacked.

We had such a great spirit at Bradford with everyone getting their share of wind-ups. John Black, a Scottish lad, never drove a car. He came to training by bike and took some stick for it. One day the lads nicked it – I think Bobby was involved – and he could not find it anywhere. John was going off his head and all the lads were saying, 'You'll see it on Sunday.' John couldn't work that one out. We had a home game on the Saturday and the match was televised on Yorkshire the next day. There was John taking a corner and above his head, 20 feet or so, was his bike, dangling by a rope from the floodlights. He hadn't even seen it during the game, but he spotted it on the highlights. He was fuming on the Monday when he came in. I think his biggest annoyance was that he had to shell out a few bob on bus fares.

You had to have a sense of humour and some chat of your own and I came in for my own trick again. I was still responsible for the contents of the skip and one away game somebody kindly swiped the towels without me knowing. I came in for the usual rollicking when we unpacked and found out my 'mistake'. There were other daft things like joke sweets and it was a good atmosphere to work in. A lot of these lads were coming to the end of their days and out to enjoy themselves while it lasted.

It was a big day when Trevor Cherry came as player-boss. I was still watching him in the Leeds side and he had just won their Player of the Year award. For someone like him to come was magnificent for the club. Terry Yorath arrived as his assistant and would also play on. To be honest we did not have the best of starts, but one consolation was that I got my first real goal, against Reading, when I came on as a sub in January 1983. It was a low left-foot shot – get in there. Trevor gave me a lot of praise afterwards, but I probably only stayed in the side because we were having problems. I had a good run – I needed one by that stage – and ended up playing 21 games in a row and scoring four goals altogether.

Trevor took stock of what he had and realised he had players who were past their best. He had to bring in free transfers and what a job he did. Greg Abbott was the first to arrive, although when he came with his glasses I thought he was a photographer. We hit it off and he stayed in digs with me for the first two years, which was more good news for mum. We had people like Peter Jackson, who was already a stalwart, and Mark Ellis, so the team was looking young again. We finished the season with wins over two big Yorkshire rivals, Sheffield United and Huddersfield, and there was tremendous optimism about the place.

Those illusions were quickly shattered as that was the summer when we nearly went bankrupt. When you are young and a bit naïve you don't notice the problems until they affect you. For a couple of weeks we went unpaid and then you knew there was trouble. The club was saved by two men who would have vastly different places in my affections, Stafford Heginbotham and Jack Tordoff. We were in the hands of the receivers and Bobby had to be sold to help settle bills. A total of eight first-teamers left. In the middle of it I signed a two-year deal on £100 a week. Where were the agents in those days? I should have sacked my mum. Out of it all Trevor did some great business, bringing in the likes of Chris Withe, John Hawley and Gary Haire. After a shocking start we put together a club record run of ten straight wins. We could even afford champagne when we stopped over after beating Exeter and had a couple of nights at Torquay. From the depression came great hope and the club's spirit carried on.

The club could have cashed in on me at the time. Liverpool were strongly linked. It must have been because of the way I could carry skips. Newcastle tried too but Trevor said he would only swap me for Kevin Keegan. At last there was some money around and the club bought Bobby back in November. He hadn't made it at Derby, so he had something to prove and he would. He also played a part in the first tragedy the club was to be involved in.

One night coming through the Midlands we hit a patch of fog on the motorway and there was a terrible braking as we smashed into the back of a car. There were two kids in the back and we knew they were hurt. Bobby dashed off the bus, smashed through the back window, cutting his arms, to try to help them. Their parents were knocked out in the front seat, so it was up to Bobby. He tried to give them mouth to mouth resuscitation, but it didn't work. One died there and then, the other in hospital a week later. We were all low for a while about it, but I will always think of how Bobby showed his big heart.

The team was relying on him too. He hit it off with John Hawley and they scored plenty. In that ten-game spell we banged in 36. Bob was the experienced man to help us youngsters. He was sensational. One thing he did not like was not scoring. We were six up against Wigan within an hour once and Bob had Mark Ellis against a wall at the end telling him his crosses were rubbish because he hadn't got one of the six goals.

For all the good work on the field – we finished seventh in the end – there were still snags off it. The floodlights fell over and poor Trevor had as many problems off the park as on it. It was to be the story of his time at Bradford. He spent more time in dealing with the board and working within budgets and not enough in training. That was where Taff Yorath was his strength. He was one of the lads.

We were recognised for our record run at a function that ended in total embarrassment for yours truly. Lawrie McMenemy, one of the top bosses of the time, was the guest speaker and we were all there in our smart clothes. It was the first time I would taste whisky and the last. I was at the table between Peter Jackson, Mark Ellis and Bobby. Ces won a bottle of whisky in the raffle but was a non-drinker, so Bob claimed it. I had never drunk whisky in my life, but the night was good and I took one. I had it with lemonade but still didn't like it. Any time I turned around I didn't know that Jacko was slipping straight shorts into my drink. Being club captain and a responsible man he was setting me up. Mark was tossing his in the plants, while Bobby and Jacko were sneaking more and more into my glass and I was not in a state to notice. Thirty minutes later the bottle had gone and so were my brains. Every time Lawrie spoke and finished a sentence this drunken bum was cheering, 'Hear, hear, Lawrie.' That drunken bum was me. For the next few months I had the nickname 'Hear, hear, Lawrie' and I could hardly complain. Trevor wasn't happy with Jacko and as for me I have never been near whisky since – I can't even smell the stuff.

The next day we went to training at Scholemoor on a big artificial pitch. I was ill, but tried to put a brave face on it. I tried to trap a ball in the first minute and missed it, putting my leg into the wall instead. There was a hush. I thought I was in for a rocket. But Taff just collapsed with laughter and called off training on the spot. I think they realised I had broken a record myself the night before. I couldn't have been too badly damaged because I scored the equaliser against Oxford the Saturday after.

I played in all 46 games that season and scored five goals. I was being linked with a lot of top clubs, but it was only flattering. I was happy with my game and the club and settled at home. The next season brought John Hendrie, another shrewd signing from Coventry, like Greg Abbott. We had the camaraderie, we had no big stars, the boss had pulled off a couple of gem signings with Dave Evans coming from Halifax too. A lot of these lads were gagging for a second chance while others like me had a feel for the club. It was going to be a massive season for me and the team. You could sense it.

John moved in with Greg and me for a while and we all went about together. It was one out, all out. One for all, all for one. It showed on the pitch as we put Middlesbrough out of the Milk Cup and drew Newcastle. That was going to plan too until Glenn Roeder gave me a showing up. He had this trick of lifting his leg up to fake a step over the ball, sending you the wrong way and shuffling past. We were 2–1 down and there with not long left when he came at me. I saw the first step and refused to fall for it, but then he did it a second time with the other leg. I went for that one, he skipped past me, played a one-two and stuck it in. Taff asked me what happened and I said, 'You never mentioned the double shuffle.' Taff admitted it was just great skill. Chris Waddle scored in the return leg to put them through but at least we gave a good account of ourselves. I must have done something right because Jack Charlton, Newcastle's manager, tried to buy me. The club wanted £150,000 but they would not pay. I wasn't bothered as I felt I was young enough to move later and enjoying myself too much. It wasn't lack of ambition, I just thought we were going the right way.

The bigger shock was to find that Dave Sexton was watching me for England's under-21 team. So were Scotland but that is another chapter.

Chapter 3

Hi, Jock Stein here

I didn't realise that Scotland were watching me thanks to my dad. Young Andy McCall had gone to Woodside school in Burnbank, Hamilton, with a certain Jock Stein. Being footballers they knew each other although my dad was two years younger. He sent him a letter, telling Mr Stein I was eligible to play for Scotland through him and that I was a Tartan Army member with international service on the terraces. Jock wrote back to him and told him they would look into it. By chance Alex Ferguson, the Scotland coach at the time, had seen me have a decent game at Preston and the report was good. All it needed then was confirmation that I wanted to play for the land of my father. Jock asked a journalist to check me out and I said I would love to play for Scotland, no problem. I never gave it much thought. There was so much in the paper about me that I reckoned it was just another story that would come to nothing.

Then the day came. I was picked for Scotland's under-21s one Monday morning and was stunned when I heard the news after training. I was overjoyed, but there was no one around to talk to, so I sat in the bath alone and tried to take it in. I was so proud and pleased and then the secretary, Terry Newman, put his head round the door and said: 'We've got good news. England want you as well.' I went from delight to being shocked and exasperated. I couldn't believe it. For the next hour and a half I was frantic. Trevor Cherry came in and asked me what I thought. He and Taff knew I was a Scot at heart, but they were saying I was born in England and should pick them. Then they said Scotland were only picking home-based players and there were no Anglos in it. Taff said I wouldn't fit in up there because of that. He said it was more prestigious to play for England and even Brian Edwards chipped in to tell me what a great honour it was to play for England. There were so many things for and against, but I kept thinking I could never pull on an England jersey against Scotland.

It was a nightmare. The secretary kept coming in and asking for an answer. The press were now waiting outside to speak to me too. The phone was going at the club with calls from Dave Sexton and Alex Ferguson wanting to know which one I had picked. The lads were all chipping in, imagine playing for England at Wembley. Then Trevor said it would be difficult up there because of my accent. Strangely that rang true as I had always taken stick for that when I went 'home' for my holidays. That was a big thing for me, silly as it sounds now. I was quite a sensitive kid and going up there talking with a Yorkshire accent was a problem. It still felt that way in later years. People look at you slightly differently when you talk like that and I was a bit self-conscious.

I was just a young lad. I tried to get hold of my dad, but couldn't track him down. I rang my mum at work and she was proud and wanted me to pick Scotland but didn't want to sway me. She accepted that the football people probably knew best. This was a totally horrendous position to be in. At 12 noon I was a Scotland player, by 1.15 p.m. I had chosen England. I was in a trance. Going home I wasn't happy. I had time to think it over and knew I had made the wrong decision. If I had 24 hours to sleep on it there would have been only one choice. There were so many arguments in my head and I was in tears several times trying to come to terms with it.

At 7.30 that night the phone went at home. It had been going all day and my mum was fielding most of the calls,

Everyone had been on, newspapers and friends. I was getting sick of talking about it, it just wasn't funny. 'It's Jock Stein on the phone,' my mum said. 'Yeah, sure,' I replied. I picked up the phone and snapped: 'All right, Jock. Who is it?' I thought there was no way Jock Stein had tracked me down to a house in Leeds. I was shaking when I heard the voice and realised it was Jock Stein. I remember he asked me if I was sure I had made the right decision. I said: 'I really don't know.' He said: 'I think you've made the wrong one, but all the best in your career. Good luck, son.' Right then the tears were down my face and my hands were quivering. It was the one and only time I spoke to Jock Stein. My mum thought I had heard bad news. It was. I never slept a wink that night. I kept thinking what if I have to play against Scotland. It would be impossible.

What really hurt was finding out later that the reason I was pressurised into picking England by Bradford's officials was that they thought it would increase my transfer value. Terry Yorath admitted it later. I had heard it whispered but never believed it. In reality I am sure Trevor and Brian wanted me to play for England because they were English. Taff wasn't, so he had no excuse. They were just looking on me as a commodity they could sell and it didn't appear to matter that I had been put through hell.

The day after my decision I was still in a spin on the team bus going to Plymouth. Everybody was saying I had made the right choice. My brother and sister were disappointed but backed me. My mum and dad were probably the same but never said much. 'Whatever you think, son,' they chorused. John Hendrie was the only one who said I got it wrong. He gave some friendly stick. 'Call yourself a Jock,' he cracked. That hurt a bit as well. I just felt numb. It wasn't how it should be. I wasn't enthusiastic, but I tried to tell myself I had made the decision, get on with it. But if I had gone to a game that afternoon I would have been cheering on Scotland. If Allan Wells was running I would have rooted for him or David Wilkie at swimming. These people always got me going.

I can't remember a thing about the Plymouth game, it just went past me. By the weekend I was a little better. We beat

Derby and then it was off to Turkey with England. I drove down to Luton airport and still wasn't at peace with myself. You've done it now, it's not going to change. My gut knew I was wrong, but I was trying to get my head round the situation. I was nervous joining up with all these players anyway, but what made it worse was that they knew I was really a Scotland fan in the first place.

The newspapers back home had me in the team. Paul Bracewell had an injury and I was supposed to be in. But Dave Sexton named his side on the Monday and it read: David Seaman, Barry Venison, Paul Parker, Ian Butterworth, Chris Fairclough, Paul Bracewell, Ian Snodin, Trevor Steven, Gary Lund, Danny Wallace, Wayne Fereday. Bracewell did have an ankle injury and had a test on the morning of the game, so it was still close. I thought the training would be better at international level. We did some 'shadow' work on the Monday, the first team against the rest, and I remember Fereday going down to the by-line and smacking a cross into the cowfield behind the goal. 'Well done, at least you got there,' roared Mike Kelly, the under-21 coach. I thought: 'What's going on?'

Then came the game. Bracewell was fit but I've got to be honest and say I was willing to play. It was a poor match and at half-time there was no hint of changes. I was sent out to warm up behind the goal. I heard the public address system and asked what it said. 'Five minutes to go,' somebody replied. I was limbering up with Tony Cottee and then Bobby Mimms came running over and told me I was to come to the dug-out and go on. I thought this was strange. Why the hurry and why me? I wasn't going to change the course of the game. They were taking Ian Snodin off. I asked one of the blokes how long was left. He said we were in injury-time. I thought there and then that this was an insurance policy against me ever playing for Scotland. They wanted to brand me, get me on for a minute and then forget me. If I came good, great, I would be recalled, if I didn't they had put me out of ever playing for Scotland.

I decided to waste those precious seconds. I messed about

with my tie-ups, I faffed around and pretended I lost my shinpads. They were pushing me to get on. Sexton kept asking: 'Are you ready, are you ready?' It was the first time he had spoken to me. I would have accepted my fate if there were 15 minutes to go, but this was a farce. I was on my feet reluctantly, edging towards the touchline and international misery. By now I've developed a limp. The linesman was waving his flag to get the referee's attention. He blew. Oh no. What's the point for ten seconds? Everything was going through my head. Then it dawned on me – he had blown his whistle for full-time. I thought I was going on, but it was too late.

I'm there on the touchline, the linesman has checked my studs. I just turned away and headed down the tunnel with a massive weight off my shoulders. I smiled to myself and all my troubles drained away in a flash. I never said a word to anyone about it, just packed up and waited for the flight home the next day. Sexton said not to worry, there would be a next time. I had made my mind up that there never would be. From being forced into a decision I did not want to being seconds away from being used as a ploy, it all became clear to me.

I went to the Turkey game with England's big team on the Wednesday. They won 8–0 and Mark Wright and Peter Withe dished out the champagne on the way home on the plane. I was there supping with the enemy. But when I got home I knew what to do. Firstly I watched a tape of Scotland beating Spain 3–1 over and over again. Then I went to training the next day and told Trevor Cherry to get in touch with England and say it was thanks but no thanks in future. I told him I wasn't happy about the way they tried to get me on like that. I was going to be picked for the next squad against Israel in January, but there was no point. I was at peace with myself and happy at last. I never expected to get another chance with Scotland, certainly not in the immediate future. I knew I had gone against them first time. Why give a kid from Bradford City a second chance to show you up?

I took some stick in Scotland and England at the time, but it was just a bad judgement made in a short space of time. I heard later that Jock Stein had a smile when he saw I pulled out of the next England squad. However, he never did pick me again. I don't blame him. There was just that tiny chance that one day I could be in a Scotland team. I would have waited to make the over-35 side, but at least it would have felt right.

Chapter 4

Champions

The only good thing about being picked for England is that everybody knew about me and clubs started making regular scouting trips to watch our games. We went on a six-game winning run and I scored three goals along the way. There was a belief in the squad and the fans were turning out in large numbers, particularly strong and loyal away. We had a huge match against Millwall, who were top, and beat them in front of 8,800. We were flying high at the top of the league and won at Reading and Lincoln. I kept on scoring from midfield and everyone thought this was our season.

Chelsea made a £100,000 bid at the time, but it didn't bother me as I was tuned in to getting my team promoted. If anything it just raised my confidence. We were big news in Bradford and I even got asked to switch on the Christmas lights. I had to kick a giant ball into a net to flick the switch. Fortunately I didn't miss. The local radio station voted me their Sports Personality of the Year ahead of Elleray Hanley, the great Rugby League player. Swimmer Adrian Moorhouse was the young personality winner. Talk of leaving never entered my head and Trevor went on record as saying that I was simply not for sale anyway. It was a boost for the fans to know that the chairman, the management and everyone was determined to get it right without selling up. I was just chuffed they wanted to keep me so much. Money was not an issue at the time. I was on a decent wage and wasn't in a rush for a quick killing. The only hiccup was a home defeat by Doncaster on Boxing Day before we won the next three. If we had not slipped up it would have equalled our old record of ten straight wins. We won at Bolton and then beat Rotherham on New Year's Day when I put one past the England under-21 keeper Bobby Mimms, an early goal for Scotland so to speak. My big pal Mark got the winner and we were all up on the railings celebrating with the fans at the end.

In the FA Cup we thrashed Tow Law Town 7–2 with Don Goodman getting a hat-trick. Don had come through the ranks too, although he was never an apprentice. He was an electrician at the time. We drove in together and it was good to see another local boy make good, although I would not have guessed he would go on to have transfers that totalled about £2 million in his career. He is a smashing lad and one of the funniest I know. The run ended at Telford in a game that should never have been played. The pitch was hard and ice-bound, but there was a big crowd in and the police forced the ref into the decision of going ahead. We went down 2–1 but that was a blessing in the long run as it let us concentrate on the league. An old cliché but true.

There was one stage when we lost just one game in 20 and had a storming match at Hull that said it all about the team and the club. The keeper, Eric McManus, had to go off with a cut face from one of Billy Whitehurst's famous elbows and young Tony Clegg, another local boy, took the jersey and went in. He took some hammer as well, but we came through and won. That told me we had what it takes as a team and it is one of my favourite Bradford games. The next week we got thumped at Millwall to end that run and I took it worse than most.

For the first time my form was suffering and I took it to heart. I had played 100 games without a break and the boss took me aside and told me to take a rest. Miss a game? No chance. I just trained with the kids for a day or so and stayed away from the rest of the team. He thought the transfer talk and the Scotland-England thing had just caught up with me. I went away, cleared my head and his psychological trick worked. We beat Brentford in an epic on the Saturday, coming from 3–0 down to win 5–4, a match that showed the character of the side. Big Bob didn't notch, so he wasn't happy and gave John a blast for going for a hat-trick when he could have squared for him to score. 'You wee Scottish b******' were his words as he chased him up the tunnel. We beat Plymouth the week after and I mishit the winner into the bottom corner.

We clinched promotion at Cambridge in a midweek match out in the wilds with a small crowd. It was a poor first half, but we banged in four after the break with Messrs Campbell and Hawley splitting them. The party started and we had a good night back in Bradford. Going out and celebrating was part of our success. We were close and had no cliques. It was part of our make-up and certainly did not do us any harm. However, we did pay for that excess in the next two games by losing at Bournemouth and then being blitzed at home 5–2 by Reading. We still had enough points to go to Bolton needing a win to be champions. There were thousands from our place – they knew we had fought hard all season for them and appreciated it. Bob scored in the first half and I had the pleasure of bagging the second. It was the last goal we scored in the Third Division. Even Trevor, who was Mister Sober, always calm, collected and reserved, managed to get stuck into the champagne. Hawley and Campbell got the cigars out. It was great for those lads, who had seen a lot in their days and were enjoying the moment they had worked hard for. People like Eric McManus and Dave Evans, one of the best signings the club ever made, were so pleased to have won something important. Us kids just lapped it up for the first time, not realising the significance the way they did. We were so sure we were on the way up that the older boys appreciated the glory so much more.

It had been a magnificent season. I played in every game again, scored eight goals in the days when I was allowed to go into the other team's penalty box and I got in the PFA's team of the year too for the first time. We had a holiday planned for all our efforts and a civic reception lined up as well. It was the first time since 1937 that Bradford had been in the Second Division. The pride was bursting out of the city. One last home game against Lincoln to come and the celebrations could begin.

Chapter 5

Tragedy

The mention of 11 May 1985 will always put a shiver down my spine and thousands more besides. Not just in Bradford, but around the country and maybe the world. What was to be a carnival, a gala, turned into one of the worst tragedies in British football. I remember coming out before the game and we all had cards spelling out 'Thank you, fans' which we paraded around the ground. There were loads of our people there, the atmosphere was tremendous. We could relax a bit and enjoy what had been a terrific season. The old stadium was full of joy.

It was not much of a match. Just minutes before half-time we saw smoke coming out of the main stand on the far end from the dressing-room. Fans were coming on to the park. You could not imagine what this was going to lead to. It's something I never saw before or want to again. The ref stopped the game as people came on to the pitch. In seconds there was smoke drifting over the playing area. We were told to go to the dressing-room fast. We left the park not knowing what was going on out there. When we got to the dressing-room panic had set in. Terry Yorath screamed out to us to get what we could, leave the ground and get outside. I grabbed my blazer and shoes and got out of the building into the street. I still had my strip on underneath, nothing else.

By this time, in only a matter of a minutes, there was a dark cloud covering us. I sneaked back into the ground by a side entrance and saw what had happened. The whole stand was engulfed by flames. Police and firemen were all over the park. One officer appealed to me to ask the couple sitting on the pitch who were in a state of shock to leave the ground at the other side. But I wanted to see what was happening to my family.

Hundreds were just looking on in amazement but all I could think about was my family. I was frantic. There was my mum, my fiancée, Liz, my brother Les, my nephew John, who had celebrated his tenth birthday the day before, and twin nieces Karen and Jane who were in their teens. I knew they were all in Block A with the complimentary tickets. That was the opposite end from where the fire started. I thought they would be all right. But my dad and his girlfriend Joan were right in the middle of the stand. I peered into the stand but could not see any sign of anyone being involved in the disaster. It was all going on out of view, but I didn't know.

I rushed out of the ground and into the street again, bumping into players who were passing on messages about who was where. Peter Jackson's dad was okay, someone said they had seen my mum and she was fine. We were milling around the back of the Midland Road stand in a daze and in chaos. After what seemed like ages I found my niece Jane, one of the twins. She was in tears. She explained that she had gone to the tea bar at the back of the stand for my mum and Les and sister Karen. In the panic a man in a uniform, that's all she could remember, shoved her out of a door at the back. She was pleading to get back in, not knowing the extent of the fire. If she had got back in she would almost certainly have died.

Now it was a two-man hunt. Finally we met Liz and John who had luckily left for the players' lounge, in relative safety, minutes before the fire began. There was easy access to the streets from there. We went out and found my mum, Les and niece Karen, who had a tearful reunion with Jane. By that stage it was ten minutes after the search began but it felt like forever. That left my dad to be found. Although he was 60, he was a fit and young 60. At that moment no one knew there were casualties never mind fatalities. The word went round for players and staff to meet in the pub at the top of the road to get organised and sort ourselves out. Even in the lounge of the pub, watching what was going on with the TV now beaming back pictures of Bradford to the country, we were only hearing that there were no deaths and everyone appeared to have escaped. I don't blame them, as no one could see what was happening out of sight in the darkness at the back.

Over an hour later I went to the car park 20 yards away from the stand. The firemen seemed to have gained control. I asked a policeman if everybody was okay. His face was white, paler than I had ever seen, and he said: 'Those who could get out got out.' It was only when I looked at him as he spoke that I knew there had been real horror.

I put the keys in the ignition and the whole car was boiling. The windscreen was roasting. I packed in the rest of the family and we drove back to Leeds. On the radio it was saying that the death toll was rising minute by minute. When we got to my sister Janette's I rang my dad's house and even though there was no answer I had no reason to panic. We had gone to the game separately, he would probably be making his way back slowly. After half an hour of trying, Les and I decided to go back to the ground. It was only ten miles and 20 minutes away and we looked up the spot where my dad usually parked his car, a little space in the back streets which he had arranged for home games. It wasn't there, so I took it he must have been away back home by now. Only later he told me the crowd was so big that day that he couldn't get into his normal place.

Just to be sure we contacted a policeman and asked where the casualties had been taken. We went straight to Bradford's Royal Hospital and there were queues of people around, all in Bradford shirts and colours, all anxiously waiting in reception. We asked a nurse if there was an Andy McCall on the list. I don't know if I wanted him to be on it or not. It didn't dawn on me that if he wasn't the chances were he would be dead. She told us quickly that there was an Andy McCall, but that he had been sent to Pinderfields Hospital in Wakefield. That was where the more severely injured had been sent. That was the special burns unit. Les and I jumped back into the car in a state of turmoil. The 25-minute drive to Wakefield was hard, one of the worst journeys of my life. Les was trying to assure me dad was okay, not to worry. I was still in my kit and blazer but I didn't think anything about it. We got to Pinderfields and a nurse told us straightaway that my dad was all right, the burns would only be superficial and that he would be fine. I hugged her and broke down. She said to wait for 15 minutes while they cleaned him up before we would be able to see him.

Worse was still to come. A nurse led us to the ward and stopped between two beds, saying, 'There's your dad.' I looked at the first bed, the one on my left, and saw this poor man who was totally unrecognisable. He had blisters all over his face, a sight I will never forget. I thought that was my dad and just screamed. A second later a voice came from the right, 'Son, son, I'm over here. I'm okay.' I turned and there was my dad. He was lying there with both hands wrapped in bandages. His face was covered in orange ointment they had used for the burns and his head was bandaged at the top. But he was able to speak. I have never known relief like it. We sat for a while with him explaining what had happened. He had taken Joan to get out of the back of the stand, but found the doors were closed. In the mayhem he managed to fight his way down to the front of the stand and over the wall to safety. He was obviously mentally scarred by it. He told us it had been every man for himself and sheer panic took over. I didn't ask too hard what he meant. In the scramble people were standing on each other.

In the next few weeks I visited my dad day and night. He needed skin grafts on his hands and the top of his head. It was a long and painful process. I also became strongly attached to the other nine or so severe casualties on the ward. I didn't know them, but I couldn't get them out of my head. The man in that bed on the left unfortunately died a few days later, that was how close to home this whole awful business was to me. All the other patients showed remarkable courage. I remember taking the Third Division trophy in just as a gesture really. Or so I thought. I was amazed that the sight of this piece of silverware could lift so many people who had gone through so much. They had all suffered and yet, apart from the strength of their families, what kept them going was their love for Bradford City. The thought of seeing us play in the Second Division gave them that extra target for recovery. There were powerful emotions at the time, quite astounding. Football then should have been the furthest thing from their minds, but yet it was such a big part of them. There were some who were bitter – anyone who lost three generations of a family would be – but the overall feeling was one of an incredible bond between us.

One couple, Duncan and Muriel Firth, stick with me particularly. Tragically, Muriel died in hospital after an operation, but Duncan was a tremendously strong man and managed to cope. He got over his injuries and I have met him many times since. He was one of the first people back at Valley Parade when we returned. He also became a writer for newsletters helping people to handle personal tragedies and loss. A remarkable man.

The players went around all the hospitals in Bradford and the surrounding areas. The response from the patients, who just wanted pictures taken with them, was unbelievable. The majority were so cheered up it was amazing. I also visited Joan, my dad's girlfriend, who was giving cause for concern at first. She improved, but like my dad and hundreds of others the mental scars were as bad as the physical ones. Princess Diana also visited Pinderfields one day and it was one of the few afternoons when I couldn't make it. She flew in by helicopter unannounced and I ticked off my dad, telling him that he should have phoned to say she was coming. Her visit cheered everyone up and showed just what a national issue the fire disaster had become.

The chairman insisted we went to the funerals, but he

didn't have to persuade us. I had never been to one in my life, but for the next few months they were regular events. I went to Muriel's, just on my own, and it was a day that will stay with me forever.

You try to block it out, but every time you hear of a disaster, any disaster, it all comes flooding back. I think of the consequences, the suffering, the people who have died and the ones near them who are going through all that again. To be in the middle of something quite as devastating leaves wounds and pictures that will never go away.

Since then my dad has never been to Bradford. He was invited to the opening when we played an England XI but thought long and hard and could not manage it. There was too much there to remind him. He could only manage to see me once playing for Everton in three years and that was enough for him. It was too much of a mental effort and he never felt comfortable. He only forced himself to see me play for Rangers once in my first six years there. Fortunately, recently he was able to come and see me play for Rangers. He is now more at ease about it and feels happier.

The only positive thing to come from the fire was the deep unity it created between the players, the club and the community. Deep down there was a desire within us all to repay those fans who had lost so much and gone through such tragedy. It brought home to me what football can mean to people. You never knew quite what to say on those hospital visits and yet just being there could lift spirits.

The people who came back to Valley Parade were proud as well as brave. I don't know if I could have been among them if I had lost anyone that day. Your mind throws up all sorts of equations and I believe I could never have set foot there again if one of my family had died. I was a fortunate one.

The help and care the hospital staff gave not only to my dad but every other patient was tremendous and I will always be grateful for the skill of the surgeons.

Chapter 6

So near, so far, so long

The 1985–86 season was a strange one to go into. We signed goalkeeper Peter Litchfield, Adie Thorpe came from non-league and Martin Singleton joined from Coventry. The star signing was Arthur Graham from Leeds, another of my old heroes. The pre-season was a nightmare. All summer had been spent at functions and fund-raising events for the fire victims. I was still living in Leeds and for all the rivalry between the two we had a great response from working men's clubs, schools and the like when we were collecting money. All over the country people were rallying round.

When we got back to the club it was very difficult for Trevor and Taff to get our minds back on football. We had been to funerals, I was visiting my dad and the summer had not been a break at all. Trevor got us together and said we had to start concentrating again for those people. We owed it to everyone else to sort ourselves out and represent them properly. It was hard to think straight – we had new players but had lost our home. We would be playing at Leeds, Huddersfield and eventually Odsal Stadium in Bradford. Trevor said we were like gypsies only without the earrings. Taff always had a word or two that counted and he told us about a letter he had received from a young girl whose dad had died. She said she was not bitter, but just wanted us to do well for him and get back to Valley Parade. That summed up exactly how we felt.

The only bright spot of the pre-season was beating Manchester United 3–1 in a friendly. They had some of their big stars like Frank Stapleton out and Ron Atkinson was glowing about me afterwards.

We started off at Carlisle and that was when the feeling came back. We stopped for lunch at a village on the way up and it was full of people in Bradford colours. It was a bright day and just felt like a new beginning. Everyone was with us and we could at last look to the future. What a lift that gave us and we won 2–1 with Bobby scoring twice. Reality hit us as we lost two away games and then came 'home' to Elland Road. It was strange playing there with just 7,000 of a crowd, a decent following but small in that huge ground. It was eerie, but we managed to beat Stoke. The players liked Leeds Road, Huddersfield, better and we won all six of the games we played there against the likes of Hull and Barnsley.

We went back to Valley Parade occasionally for training, only after they had tidied it up. It was hard with the backdrop of where the old stand was. Every time you looked over the memories were still there. It was upsetting to train there. However, 99 per cent of the supporters wanted to go back and the players were the same.

It wasn't until 14 November that we came back to Bradford to play at Odsal. It was only to help our fans travel less, but if the players had had the choice we would have stayed at Huddersfield. At least it was a football ground. Odsal was just a big bowl, a Rugby League ground with a speedway track round it and one covered end for the fans. It had everything against it being a football ground. Those were difficult times for the club. We kept hearing that the move back to Valley Parade was delayed and we were struggling in the league. It all went together.

I also had the chance to play at Elland Road in a 'real' game that season for the first time when we played Leeds. Peter Lorimer scored with a rare header and we lost. I had waited so long for that chance and it was a disappointment. It was like that at the time. I also ended an unbroken run of about 140 games with an injury in December when I turned quickly and felt a pain in my foot. I tried to play through it, but x-rays showed I had broken a bone. I was in plaster for a week or so and only missed four games. One consolation was that I had Christmas off and celebrated New Year's Eve in true style, getting plastered in more ways than one.

We had always been on the up and up and for once this was a down part. Lesser sides would probably have gone under, but we had that spirit and faith and an aim to keep the club going at that level for the fans' sake. We finished 13th which was good considering everything we went through. The fire had been hard to get over and you could throw a blanket over that season for me and forget it. One of the few bright spots was the arrival of big Ian Ormondroyd, Sticks as we called him, who made a big impact not just with his height but also his ability. He was a local lad again, from Thackley, and was a left-winger at first, quick and with massive strides. He was always going to be dangerous. Ian made a living out of the game and almost surprised himself by doing that. He went on later to Aston Villa for £650,000. On a personal note Lawrie McMenemy tried to buy me for Sunderland for £200,000. He must have forgiven me for that night I kept shouting 'Hear, hear, Lawrie'. But Cherry was unhappy because it was in the papers and the fee was put up because of it.

My own form had been all right that season, but I did not see that as an escape. I must have been quite hard on myself because I was voted second in the Second Division ratings in a magazine, behind Danny Wilson of Brighton. He was a worthy winner because he gave me an absolute chasing when we played down there. He taught me a lesson. I was supposed to be man-marking him and within 25 minutes he had scored a hat-trick. That was the worst grilling I took that season and I learned a lot from it. On the transfer front I had pledged myself to stay with the club until we got back to Valley Parade at least. The trouble was that move was going slowly.

I believe that if we had played that season at Valley Parade on the back of promotion and with the new faces we had brought in we would have gone very close to promotion first time out. Unfortunately, it was a dream that had become a nightmare.

The strain took its toll on Trevor – he had to deal with it all behind the scenes. For Taff it wasn't so bad, he had the training, but Trevor was always at meetings and it was draining his enthusiasm. There was some bitterness about him and you could see signs of splits growing between him and the board. We were not used to that and it was something else that put a shadow over the season.

The financial side of the club was obviously under strain with our nomadic existence and rebuilding the ground and for the first time I found out they would sell me, which came as a huge shock. I came within 90 minutes of moving on at the start of the 1986–87 season. Aberdeen boss Alex Ferguson and assistant Archie Knox came down to a West Riding Cup tie at Halifax. It was just a couple of days before their deadline for signing players for Europe and the papers all said the deal was on. But more importantly Trevor told me they were coming and something might happen. I was puzzled as I had never been available before. I ran out at The Shay and it was a strange feeling to know two pairs of eyes in particular were watching me. There weren't many there so I could even pick out where they were sitting. They stood out like sore thumbs. It was about as official as you get – I was on my way if I did well. I thought I did okay but it was a tame pre-season game and not what they were used to watching.

However, Trevor told me to be at the club early next morning as I could be sold. I went home thinking, 'Whose decision is this?' Aberdeen were flying high at the time and it would have helped my Scotland cause, but I was committed to staying with Bradford until we went back to Valley Parade. I thought the club must be needing the money, but why me? I wasn't particularly happy that the next day I could be an Aberdeen player. I had no time to think about it again, just like the Scotland thing. Trevor was saying it would be a good move to go from a club without a ground to one in the European Cup and with a manager like Alex Ferguson. As it happened when

51

I went in the next day I found out they were signing Robert Connor from Dundee instead. Trevor knew because he had been told – there was obviously a hot line between them at the time. For me Aberdeen was a long way away and I was relieved that it all fell through. People like Ian Snodin at Doncaster had moved on to bigger clubs but it didn't trouble me. I was just 22 and was content. There were whispers that I lacked ambition, but I had one. That was to return to the ground and start a new era at the club. The hopes were rising with suggestions we would make it back within a few months and finally the day came, if not soon enough.

I had another big fixture that summer too when I got married to a Leeds girl, Liz Helly. It was a big step for me and I was getting hitched at the same time as team-mate Gavin Oliver, so we decided to have a stag night together the week before. I remember it well as Scotland played Uruguay in the World Cup and I was in two minds about going out. I watched the first ten minutes and they got a man sent off, so I was sure we would win and make the second stage of the finals for the first time in history. We would surely beat ten men, so I went out to the do and when I arrived an hour later it was still 0–0 and finished that way. I was sick. It spoiled the evening for me. I got the mickey taken non-stop as England were through. Did I really ever pick them ahead of Scotland?

The new season started and stopped as I picked up injuries. I was carrying one at the start and it was a bad beginning and took us until the sixth game at Millwall to manage a win. I had to pull out after that one as the ankle got worse.

The next match was one of the most sickening experiences of my life. Leeds were at Odsal and we won 2–0. I was in the main (and only) stand opposite where all the Leeds supporters stood. They were not taking too kindly to being beaten by us with just a couple of minutes left. I could not believe what I saw. Smoke billowing from the top of the terraces from a chip van. It was being rocked by Leeds supporters and finally they tipped it over and set it alight. At a Bradford game? This couldn't be happening. The ref took the players off and panic set in again among our fans. The

Leeds people came on the pitch and were making for our side, pouring across into the seats. They wanted to get the game stopped because they were losing. It was too ugly to take in. Bradford fans who had been at the tragedy were among those who were scattered in fear. The memories came back to them and they were at risk because of a mindless mob. There was smoke, fire, it was happening again. Those Leeds thugs, a disgrace to the club, were making people flee in fear of their lives and haunted by what had gone less than two years before. They were nearer and nearer, just like a pack of animals. The police just managed to block them off and take control. Once their supporters had been taken away the game started again and finished soon after. There were not many Bradford people left either.

Weeks later they were to charge a boy with arson, setting the chip van on fire. To my disgust and amazement he was somebody who went to the same school as me, but two years younger. I won't give him the fame by repeating his name. It was a shocking coincidence that I knew him.

All the years before I had been home and away with Leeds and supported them wherever they played. It was only when we came on level terms in the league that I had looked on them differently, as rivals for the first time. I wanted them to do well in every game apart from when they met us. But after that day the feelings I had for them turned to disgust. I was so ashamed, especially when I knew who was involved. I vowed to myself I would never ever join Leeds if I had the chance presented to me. It would have been too much like kicking all those Bradford fans in the teeth. Over the years to come there were times when I could have moved there but I remembered that day and that horror and never considered it as an option. When I was a kid it was the club I dreamt of playing for. I would have done anything to wear that jersey. But there was no way I could let down or betray Bradford's fans after that incident. I was embarrassed, upset and felt awful about the whole business. To be fair so were all the staff and players of Leeds United. They were apologising to everyone they met. So were the board and the genuine fans.

It was also to be Bobby Campbell's last game for the club. He was sold to Wigan after that. Only four games later we sold Peter Jackson to Newcastle for £250,000. It was obvious to me that was the sum they had to raise and why they had considered moving me out to Aberdeen just a couple of months before. It was such a disappointment to lose a character like Bobby from the club. He stood for so much we stood for, a real giant and a great friend in good times and bad. At least he was coming towards the end of his career, but losing the skipper was a body blow. Jacko was also an inspiration and you couldn't imagine the team without him. He was a great partner and close pal of Dave Evans and we only found out how important he was when he left. He had confidence in his ability and although he was a bit of a poser he was such a superb ambassador for the club at a difficult time.

I came back a couple of weeks later and we beat Reading 3–0. We got the news we were going home and it was just as well because we were sinking fast. If we had not gone back to Valley Parade we would have gone down that season without trace. It was all getting too much. I took over as captain from Jacko – it was a great honour to be made skipper at 22. But the big news was the return to the ground. We went down a few times to look around and get a feel for it again. Bit by bit they had put the place back together.

The stadium was reopened on 14 December 1986 by Justice Sir Oliver Popplewell. We met an England select team and the club, the chairman in particular, did well to get some big names together. We won 2–1, but that didn't matter. After 18 months we were home and the fans turned out in force, 15,000 of them, and that settled any arguments about playing at Valley Parade again. People like Kevin Keegan, John Barnes and Peter Shilton all played and I got Peter Reid's jersey at the end. I needed an England strip as I had given away my two from the under-21 trip. One went to my old pal Greg Abbott and the other to the fire appeal. The new top was later going to be for my daughter Carly. It was a great occasion, with Jacko, Bob, John Hawley and Eric McManus all returning.

I just hoped this would be the start the team needed. But

our first game was a defeat by Derby on Boxing Day and it was not the surge we wanted. The day after we went to Huddersfield and got hammered 5–2 – the boss pulled me in afterwards and called me a 'headless chicken', which was my first real rollicking. He said I was trying to do too much and my form was suffering. I disagreed but looking back he was right. Because I was captain I was trying to do everyone else's job for them instead of sticking at my own. Trevor brought in old Maurice Lindley, who was respected at the club, to have a word with me. He was our scout but he had been watching me to see what was wrong, they were that concerned.

Sadly Trevor was sacked just into the New Year. Taff had already gone to manage Swansea. He had been a big part of the team, but wanted to be a number one. Terry Dolan had stepped up from youth team boss to be Trevor's assistant and he took over on a temporary basis. I was shocked at the sacking although the results had been bad – we had not won for eight games. It must have been hard for Trevor to take after all he had been through. For 18 months he had been in charge of a team of nomads. We were back home and he only had a couple of games at Valley Parade. I think it was more of a relief to him when he went. All the problems and stress left a mark, they mounted up on him. He kept himself to himself, not one of the lads, a bit reserved and completely the opposite to Taff, which is why they worked so well together. It is no surprise to me that Trevor never showed a hunger to go back into management. He probably had had enough in one job. He had taken enough and went instead into other fields where he was successful. What he went through left such a bad taste that he was put off management for good.

Terry Dolan came in as caretaker for an FA Cup tie at Oldham when I equalised, which is something I never let my Rangers pal Andy Goram forget. He just kept out a 15-yard header from me on that artificial surface they had and I followed through to score the rebound, which I have gone through hundreds of times with him since. We played a new 5–3–2 system under Dolan and it was working. We thumped Millwall 4–0 for our first home win at Valley Parade with Mark

Ellis getting a couple. Then two days later we battered Oldham 5–1 in the replay – we were five clear at half-time and that was a result that guaranteed Terry got the job. We also drew Everton in the next round. The next game at Plymouth was the only time I ever scored two goals in a game for Bradford, but we still lost in injury-time. We had a packed house for the Everton game and were unlucky to lose 1–0 with Snodin scoring. I was man of the match, which was some consolation.

It was a fairy-tale for Terry. He had come from nowhere to be boss, a job he always wanted. He fully deserved his chance and with his mate Stan Ternent he brought a new style on and off the pitch. Terry was laid-back to the point of falling over, while Stan was quiet but got stuck in with the lads on the training ground. He was aggressive and a motivator as he has shown at other clubs when he went on to be manager himself. The team now had a local lad, Karl Goddard, signed from Manchester United, and Brian Mitchell, bought from Aberdeen, as up-and-down wing-backs. It was the break-up of the old side. It was now Dolan's signings and tactics with John Hendrie moved from the wing to inside up front.

We were still struggling and the key arrival was Ron Futcher from Oldham. We had to give them big Ormondroyd in exchange on loan, but we needed Ron's wisdom at a tough time. We also off-loaded Don Goodman for £50,000 to West Brom. He was never Dolan's cup of tea although we could have got fortunes if he had stayed with us. Futcher made us forget all that and was just the man we needed. We made chances and he was a predator. He was also a character, a mercenary who never stayed anywhere long but very popular at our place. Futch spoke his mind, but he was precious to us that season and beyond. We finished well and were optimistic that good times were ahead when we lost only once in the last ten.

That season ended so well that other clubs were watching me again. Arsenal were in strongly and even Celtic had been linked. it had been a survival battle but the buzz was about the place again. Because we had struggled people thought I would be leaving, but nothing was further from my mind. I had played against the likes of Peter Reid in the FA Cup and I knew what I wanted. I wanted to be up against these guys every week, but playing for Bradford. I knew bids were turned down, but there was something special about this dream. I heard about the big wages, but I wasn't having my head turned.

I was also back in the international picture. Andy Roxburgh was Scotland's boss and had been to our games, although every time he or his scout Craig Brown had come I was below average. Roxburgh had a different attitude towards me than Jock Stein and didn't have to ask twice when he picked me for the B team against France at Aberdeen. Nothing is straightforward and we had a game at Sunderland that same night vital to our survival. We had just beaten them 3–2 at home and were almost level on points. Terry tried to get the fixture changed, but it wasn't possible so I missed out on the Scotland match. I pulled out and Ian Wilson from Leicester came in, made a big impact and was later to join Everton in the space of a few weeks. I must admit I was jealous when I saw that he also stayed in the Scotland squad and went on to the big team. That was my place he had taken. Willo even turned out against England at the end of the season at Hampden in a game we won 1–0 thanks to Richard Gough. I had missed all that, but at least we did beat Sunderland 3–2 again and I got one, a result that put them on the way down and just about saved us. However, it had at least broken down the Scotland barrier and I was accepted at last, forgiven for what I had done before.

Bradford won seven of the last nine games and finished tenth, a superb effort considering what had been a poor start and a change of management. That was the platform for the big push to come – the next season could not come quickly enough. I believed in the team and we all thought we could have a real proper go next time. The summer break was also to play a major part in that story and take a sad toll on the chairman.

As a reward for our season we went to Magalluf in June

1987, a trip that brought everybody together. John Hendrie was out of contract and could have left. I had a year left. So the chairman wanted to stop any thought of us leaving by coming on the trip and personally sorting us out with new deals, the best the club had ever given. Everyone was on a high, but we felt John would go. The chairman saw it differently and wanted us both for the push. He sat John down and told him to give it one more year, this was to be the season we would do it. John was convinced and then the chairman told me he had committed himself and the same money was there for me. I was happy with that as it was fair and it also meant the club would not be screwed at a tribunal if I left at the end of the season. That was important to me too. There was no reason for me to sign other than him and the fact that I didn't want the club to lose out financially on me later, so it cut both ways. It really was an excellent package for Bradford. The deal also came with a covering letter from the chairman which proved he was a man of his word. It stated that there was a deal between us that if we did not get promoted I would be sold in the summer of '88 even though I would still be under contract. We both genuinely believed we would go up and I would never need that document. As far as we were concerned this was a binding agreement. Otherwise why put it in writing. Little did I know what was to follow.

The chairman, Stafford, pushed the boat out by Bradford's standards and got a bit carried away with the celebrating. It was all done over a few San Miguels on that holiday. Stafford was a diabetic and really shouldn't have been going on like he did, but he was so committed and loved the craic. He loved the atmosphere and probably enjoyed himself more on that trip than at any time in his footballing life. We didn't know he had taken ill until he came back. We only found out later he had suffered a heart attack. He probably tried to keep it from us so that it didn't dampen our spirits. By all accounts he did so much damage to his heart that he needed a by-pass operation. People put forward the theory that the heart problems were down to the fire, but in a way I would be happier to know that it was down to having a good time. I hope that doesn't sound bad, but he was such a football man that if he was to be ill I would rather he had been happy on the way. The fire did take so much out of him, the criticism he took, the funerals and the meetings he attended. He did everything that a single human being could do. That must have been stressful, but there could have been the other holiday reason. He was a player's chairman, he took a lot of flak down the years, but for us he was ideal. He went to all the games and played cards with the boys at the back. He would take your money and then lose his. He would also offer us backhanders out of his own pocket if we could beat his home-town team, Oldham. That Cup replay win must have cost him, but you couldn't take the grin off his face. He was always involved with us, not just talking football but in the company. His enthusiasm had a big bearing on my career. The majority of the lads swore by him. I can't say the same for managers as Trevor and Stafford had their fall-outs, but for me he was tremendous. When Stafford came round from his heart attack I'm told the first thing he said was, 'Thank Stuart and John for signing the contracts.' If that's true it's the nicest thing I could imagine and says everything about him. He thought more about other people and his beloved Bradford than he did about himself. We saw less and less of the chairman, though. He wasn't capable of going to games because of his health and could not get involved as heavily as he had on that trip.

One other lasting memory of Magalluf was watching Dundee United in a bar on TV in the UEFA Cup final against Gothenburg. Of course I was urging them on along with John Hendrie, but there were about 20 people at the front cheering for Gothenburg and I took it they were Swedes. At the final whistle Gothenburg held out to win and there was uproar. These guys were up singing and dancing and we just finished our beers and felt a bit disappointed. This red-haired beast then came towards the bar from among the rabble and ordered a crate of San Miguel in a strong Scottish accent. I thought I had misheard him. We left the pub and on the next day we saw the red-headed monster on the beach. Arthur Graham bumped into Jocky Scott and Drew Jarvie and they explained that the loud-mouthed Swede in Union Jack shorts and sun blisters was in fact one of their Dundee players. I still couldn't understand why they would want United to lose. I thought all Scots cheered for Scottish teams. I must have been naïve because I would later share such local passions myself and find the fiery red-head a fearless team-mate and big pal. It was, of course, John Brown.

The new season started with a 2–0 win over Swindon and I scored the first goal. The boss brought in Paul Tomlinson, a keeper from Sheffield United, and Lee Sinnott came from Watford for a record £130,000. We went to Oldham and won 2–0 and the optimism was high. We won eight of the first nine games with just one draw to break up that sequence as we led the league at one stage. Places like Stoke (my 200th league game), Huddersfield (where I scored) and West Brom (notched again) were invaded and conquered. Then we beat Middlesbrough in one of the best performances seen at the new ground. We were playing great football and scoring goals.

Injuries to Karl Goddard and Greg Abbott disrupted the side and we brought in a young full-back called Steve Staunton on loan from Liverpool. He joined in the spirit of the place and landed in trouble. Kenny Dalglish dragged him back after he was done for drink-driving one night. We went out for a few beers and someone in the bar had a grudge against a player and tipped off the police. It could have been anyone, but it was Steve who got it in the neck. Dalglish didn't see the funny side and whipped him back in disgrace. He was a good lad and went on to become a top player, although frankly you would never have guessed that at the time. We could still have done with him for longer.

The date 23 November is very special to me, being the day little Carly was born. She was due at the weekend when I travelled to Reading for a Littlewoods Cup tie and drove back in a hurry. She arrived on Monday, in time for the replay, bouncing into the world at 1.35 p.m. I never kicked a ball the next day. I was physically and mentally shattered. The only thing I did was set up Sticks Ormondroyd for the winner. Unfortunately I went out and wet the baby's head with Mark

Ellis and Bobby Campbell. I got back in the early hours and woke up soon after with a call from the hospital saying there were photographers waiting for a picture. It was the worst picture ever. I still have a couple and they are shockers, but it was well worth the hangover to see the little one.

I had always wanted my children to be born in Scotland, so they could play for the country, but that was impractical. The next best thing was if the baby was a boy to call him Scot with a middle name Tish. Thankfully Carly was a lovely little girl.

January was turbulent as we bought Mick Kennedy for a record £250,000, but the chairman quit a few days later. He moved out of the country after selling his business and settled in Jersey, so the place was never quite the same without him. He couldn't go to games as he was warned he could not cope with the excitement. Jack Tordoff took over as chairman and nothing changed immediately. We thought he had the club at heart and there was no reason to think otherwise. Things started to turn against us on the field as we lost at home to Aston Villa, then slumped at Ipswich. The only win we had in that spell was over Bournemouth. We lost badly to Leeds and Stoke and then went out of the Littlewoods at Luton. Big Tomlinson fell asleep and made a mistake that handed away a free-kick in his own box which cost a goal. I can't knock him as he had a smashing season apart from that. Defeat hurt as Luton went on to win in the Cup and there was nothing between us that night.

We went through that season with 14 or 15 players. We were lucky with injuries and suspensions. A win at Millwall, courtesy of Sticks, put us on the rails again. He was sub that day and fell over in front of their fans as he was warming up – he tripped on a rake and went full length. They tortured him with cries of 'ee-aw' but he came on and the donkey had the winning kick. After that we were on a roll. I scored against Oldham and then we had a tremendous success at Middlesbrough. Sticks got them both against giants like Gary Pallister and Tony Mowbray. We played them off the park home and away and still had to meet them again in the play-offs. Incredibly, Huddersfield beat us with Ian Banks scoring the winner to break the sequence and that result cost us promotion, to my mind. We drew at Birmingham in a game when Mark Ellis picked up a knee injury that was to end his time at the top.

My Scotland debut finally came on 22 March in an under-21 game against England as an average player. I was just 23, so I wasn't as average as my room-mate Paul Hegarty. I took great delight in telling him he was my childhood hero and it was true. Paul was a star at Hamilton when I was making those summer-holiday trips, but by then he was a good old head for Dundee United. We lost 1–0 and I got a taste of clashing with young Paul Gascoigne, who even then was hyper. He only lasted 18 minutes before going off injured but even then he was running about crazy. I saw just how keen he was to succeed in a hurry. It was a shame he went off so soon. Craig Brown and Tommy Craig were in charge of the side and England had players like Des Walker, Nigel Clough and David Rocastle in their team. We had Davie Robertson, Derek Whyte, Robert Fleck, with Kevin Gallacher and John Collins too. I got enough vibes from Craig Brown to think I was in. He sent me a letter thank and saying he was impressed with my attitude on and off the park and would hopefully see me again in the full squad.

If that was what I wanted then the events at Bradford certainly weren't. The transfer deadline came and went and we didn't strengthen the squad. Other sides were doing it, like Middlesbrough taking Trevor Senior and Aston Villa splashing out. We were competing with them on the park and yet not competing with them in the transfer market. We were doing remarkably well with a small squad, but could it last? It was only natural that we would have form dips because injuries and suspensions would catch up with us. When we wanted something fresh we didn't do anything about it. That should never have happened. Deep down we felt our best chance was going to be the play-offs which meant a total of 49 games in the league alone. Signing someone new would have helped us scrape over the line. The most galling thing, the hardest to take or understand, is that they had John and me as insurance policies. They knew they would get £1.5 million for us if they missed out. It wasn't even a gamble to invest. I can't say for sure we would have done it, but I believe we would have been closer and we couldn't get much closer than we did with what we had got. We were not given the support we deserved from the board. Two players, Keith Curle and Andy Townsend, were linked at the time – rumour had it they both came to the ground – but neither was signed. It would not have cost much, and look at what they went on to do in the game. It would have been a small investment for the return of promotion. It is only when I look back that I blame people – at the time you were just getting your head down and doing your best. We were positive, what the hell? Let's get on with it.

Terry Dolan pulled us together after deadline day and said, 'That's it, we'll do the best with what we've got.' The club was in its best position for decades, they had signed a new sponsorship deal and record profits were to be announced. The bitterness came later. We just carried on and thought someone upstairs was looking after us. We were 3–0 down at Swindon when the lights went out and saved us; we were 2–0 down in the rematch and grabbed a point. Little things like that make you believe. Then we had a cruel blow at Manchester City when we came from two down to draw but had John Hendrie sent off in a scandalous decision. He was booked and went into a 50–50 with their keeper Mike Stowell. It was fair but Stowell made a meal of it and John went off. He was to be banned for the final game at home to Ipswich that would decide our fate.

That Man City weekend was also when I got my first call to the full Scotland team, as a last-minute replacement for a friendly in Spain. I was in the 18-man squad with guys like Ally McCoist and Ian Durrant, those quiet chaps from Rangers. I got to be part of it and mixed with Gough, Mo Johnston and Roy Aitken. I sat in the stand but I felt I was getting close. The bus was stoned after the game and people were diving for cover all over the place. Coisty was first on the floor of course.

Bradford needed two wins from the last three games to go

up and we beat, sorry battered, Leicester 4–1 at our place before going to Villa on Easter Monday. It was a non-event and my job was to mark David Platt. I can honestly say he did very little in the game but then popped up with the winner, a header from a free-kick. That's the story of his career too, I suppose. So then it was down to the final match against Ipswich and we had to hope Middlesbrough lost and Villa didn't win to let us go up automatically. We were against a side with nothing to play for who went at it like men possessed. At 0–0 we heard Leicester were in front at Middlesbrough and then Greg Abbott put us ahead. Just for a few minutes we were the team going up. Ipswich made it 1–1 then went ahead but I scored a solo to pull us level. It was 'game on' until Lee Sinnott gave away the Ipswich winner and that was it. Middlesbrough lost, Villa only drew and went straight up, so a win would have done it for us.

So there was no time to think what could have been as we had drawn Middlesbrough in the play-offs and still fancied ourselves against them. They were also on the back of a form slump. They missed out worse than us as they had been safely up a few weeks before. The home leg came first – Karl Goddard scored early, Senior equalised but I got the winner to give us an advantage for the return. It should have been five or six as we cuffed them and although it was slim we were sure we had enough about us to get a result up there. It did cross my mind that we should have killed them off, but this was no time for being negative. Bernie Slaven drew them level early in the second leg and that meant extra-time. Even when they got a second we still needed one goal for penalties. The final whistle was the worst feeling ever. At the end of the game I knew that was it, we had missed out and I was leaving. We had given it everything. I threw my shirt to the fans at the end and I think they realised too that it was 'goodbye'. I wouldn't play for them again. I knew Colin Harvey was there watching me for Everton, but if we had gone up that would have meant nothing.

I sat in the bath for ages, tears streaming down my face. The recriminations started on the team bus. John had a run-in with Mick Kennedy although I barely noticed. The boys at the back were silent, but up front some poison was being laid that I was unaware of for a few weeks. The next morning things started to hit home about the way we had missed out. We had gone through so many obstacles and yet things had petered out. I started to think 'if only'. People said to look on the up side, that I would be getting promotion myself, but that's not the way I saw it. If we had gone up I would have been happy to sign a ten-year contract and stay at Bradford forever. We could have given so much back to the fans who had shown such courage and loyalty in the previous seasons. That's how strong my emotions were. I thought about transfer deadline day and Tordoff saying we should sell before buying. Futch and Leigh Palin had to go before we could bring someone in. One or two new faces would have taken us over the finishing line, I was sure of it, and it nagged away. It wasn't about gambling, it was about lack of ambition. After all these years I still feel a bitter disappointment and resentment. If I had stayed I might never have played in a Cup final or made the World Cup or gone to Rangers, but nothing would have replaced playing for Bradford at the top level.

If we had gone up the club had promised to give us a trip to Disneyland which in those days was a big deal. The lads were due to have a week on their own before the families came out for the rest of the fortnight. I believe that was all on the back of a large bet Stafford had placed at the start of the season. It was a carrot he kept dangling in front of us. He would have paid for it out of his winnings, that's the man he was. At least he liked a gamble. It could have been different if he had been in charge on deadline day. Instead the club fixed us up with a trip to Rhodes as a 'thank you' but because of all the talk about me leaving I only went for four days. It was an emotional trip, the last time I would go out with these lads. When we were away Everton bid £800,000 and the club said they wanted more. It went up to £850,000 and Terry Dolan told me they were looking for £1 million. My worry was that Everton, whom I fancied joining, would go elsewhere. I had this letter of agreement that I would be sold, but there was no price. I was in the hands of the club about that part. In the end they settled for £875,000.

When I was in Rhodes two respected officials – I will keep them anonymous – told me what the chairman had apparently said on the bus home from Middlesbrough. He had apparently said to another board member that the bright side was that they were still going to get money for John and me, and, anyway, I never really did it in the big games. I was shocked and angered by those comments. Jack, you were certainly right about the sales, you made £875,000 on a player who cost you nowt, but I resent the other part. I had scored some big goals, including two at the death. One against Ipswich could have sent us up and the other against Middlesbrough could have seen us through the play-offs. I got 13 in that last season in midfield. Since I left I scored goals in the FA Cup final, the World Cup finals, twice on my European debut for Rangers, in Scottish League Cup finals. I think they are pretty big occasions. If I had heard him say those things that night I would have had it out on the spot. But that was nothing compared to what he did to me later.

The shame of Tordoff's jibe was that it was the only sour note in my leaving. I agreed to join Everton on 9 June, but wanted to go back to the club for a final Player of the Year awards dinner. I promised I would be there and wanted to as a Bradford player. I had sorted out everything with Everton but I still went away without signing a contract. Colin Harvey was great and accepted it even though they had just missed out on signing Paul Stewart and were taking some stick in the press. That was bigger news than my signing anyway. It was a highly charged night at Bradford with all the supporters coming up to me, some pleading for another season. When I collected the two awards there was even a doubt in my own mind. I was swept up by it, I had made so many friends and they were all there that night. It was pulling on my heart-strings quite a bit. I pledged that night that I would love to go back and play for the club one day. It's still a part of me that will never leave.

The next day I went back to Everton on my 24th birthday

and signed. Eight great years to the day since I signed for Bradford I left a great club who had given me my start and provided some memorable moments. The amount of letters from well-wishers proved that they thought as much of me as I did of them. I had been linked with clubs from the age of 20 and had been accused of lacking ambition by staying. This was the time to move on. I had decided a year before to give it one final season to fulfil the dream, but it wasn't to be.

Then Tordoff came back to haunt me again. I was still to be paid the second half of a payment agreed with Stafford when I signed my deal the summer before. Being the man he was he put John and I on identical terms, down to the wages and signing-on payments. John got £500 a week and a signing-on fee of £25,000 after tax and so did 1. The only difference was that John got that on signing, while I would receive two lumps of £12,500 in July 1987 and July 1988. All tax implications were to be the club's responsibility. The club paid the first £12,500 and I was waiting on the other one. I was amazed to find they sent me a cheque for £4,172.85 which in my eyes was a shortfall of £8,327.15. I thought it was just a mistake and wrote to them but they refused to pay the rest of the money they owed to me, claiming this would take the cost to them to a gross £28,410 to find that second half of £12,500 after tax. They thought they were just due me £6,590 because it had cost them so much to pay the first £12,500 and the tax. Basically it was a cheap trick. The original deal struck between the chairman and me was for two payments of £17,500 which we worked out after tax would leave me £25,000. The club were to pay the tax and I was to receive the two £12,500 payments on two dates.

Regrettably I had to take my old club to the Football League. I called in the PFA to represent me. The money was really irrelevant, it was the principle and the fact that they were doing this to me. I had brought them in £875,000 and they were arguing about £8,000. I went to an appeal at Bramall Lane with a letter from Stafford, fully supporting my claim and detailing all we had agreed. Astonishingly the committee voted 2–1 against me and we lost. Mick McGuire of the PFA lodged an immediate appeal. I don't know what their reasons were, although I suspect one of their members did not get on with Stafford, but I wasn't accepting the verdict. It wasn't until October when they finally shared my point of view. There was no new evidence, just the same argument and the solid reasons they were given in the first place. It had to come down on my side.

This all left a bad taste. The chairman even went public and told the local paper I had made £80,000 in my last season, trying to make me look a money-grabber. What that didn't mention was that it included bonuses, all in our contracts and payable because we spent most of the season in the top three. They were getting good gates, so we were rewarded for it. Nobody complained at the time. We agreed those incentives in advance and it was legitimate. We were playing to full houses and deserved our cash. The chairman even said they would appeal against the decision. I think the fans saw through the propaganda and knew the score.

The cheque finally came along with a letter from the chairman. It read: 'Dear Stuart, After studying the report of the appeal hearing I am satisfied with their findings. A chat with me months ago, explaining your side of the situation, would have avoided this misunderstanding. Enclosed is a cheque for £8,327.15. We will shake hands the next time we meet. Yours sincerely, Jack Tordoff.'

This annoyed me more than anything. My side of the situation had been made clear from the word go. The club knew about it and were told many times, that's why the PFA were called in. They accepted defeat but it was their fault it ever happened.

It wasn't until many years later that I bumped into Jack Tordoff, sadly at Stafford's funeral. We politely shook hands, but inside I will always be sickened by the dealings over the money. Even worse I point the finger at the board for failing the club in that final push. Now when I meet Bradford fans or players from that era it is the major talking point, how we came so close and yet so far.

Chapter 7

In with the big boys

There was only one club I was going to join when I left Bradford and that was Everton. There were others mentioned, but Everton had made their interest known and were definitely keen. At the time they were one of the five biggest clubs around and had won the championship the year before. Well-informed people had told me the move was on and Terry Dolan told me they had bid when we were away after the season finished. It was ideal, nearly everybody in the side was an international and it wasn't a big upheaval to move across to Merseyside either.

I was so sure about the move that I didn't even bother taking an adviser. I met Mike Lyons, the Everton legend who was a coach under Colin Harvey, and he made me feel at home. My mind was made up really. I spoke to Stafford for advice before I went over and he told me not to accept the first offer they gave me, even though it would be bigger money than I had ever seen, but just to wait and see if there was more. I also consulted my solicitor Stephen Lownsbrough of Nelson and Co who has helped and advised me throughout my career and been a good friend down the years. In the end I held out for £50 a week more, that's how hard I was to get. It was a football decision with one of the main factors being the chance to play with Peter Reid. So I signed on my 24th birthday and went on to a wage that almost trebled my old Bradford money.

Colin Harvey spent big that summer, bringing in Neil McDonald from Newcastle, Pat Nevin from Chelsea and finally Tony Cottee from West Ham for £2 million. We were all to become close friends. I now had to focus on being an Everton player and making an impact in the top flight. Things started well and I scored a beauty from 30 yards in a pre-season game in Switzerland. It was to be the exception rather than the rule. I warned them not to expect that every week. It was good to go away with so many new boys and we all mixed well. We went to Ireland and played Drogheda, but before we flew home the assistant boss, Terry Darracott, ordered us for a meeting. I thought it was more training, but instead we went into the bar and had a sing-song for a couple of hours. There seemed to be a really good spirit with Dave Watson doing his version of *Two Little Boys* and Ian Snodin singing *King of the Road*. We had a few beers and I went home thinking this was a magic club where everyone got on.

We kicked off the season against Newcastle and it could not have been a better start. There was a bus over from Bradford to see me and John Hendrie, who was making his debut for the Geordies. TC got a goal after 35 seconds and went on to get a hat-trick, I looked around and saw top players like Neville Southall, Watson, Kevin Ratcliffe, Reidy, Graeme Sharp and Kevin Sheedy and thought this will do me. We won at Coventry in midweek and were top of the league.

I found a house quickly in Southport and all was going well until the next game with Luton at home. I had a great chance late on, one I would normally take, but I froze and fluffed it. That probably affected my confidence as we lost 2–0 and I had seen a first goal and the points go. If that had gone in, who knows? I never did score in the league that season and look back on that moment in horror. I did get one against Bury in the League Cup a week later which was relief but a false dawn. As luck would have it we drew Bradford on a night of mixed emotions. The fans were great and gave me a reception that brought a lump to my throat, but our team were outplayed. We got a real doing and lost 3–1.

After a bright start we were struggling in mid-table and the boss decided to break up the championship-winning team. Gary Stevens and Derek Mountfield had already gone, Adrian Heath would leave and sadly Peter Reid was on his way after New Year. I had looked forward to playing with him and forging a partnership just as he had done with Paul Bracewell, but it wasn't to be.

Frankly I never did myself justice. I was too much in awe of the international names in the side. When I was at Bradford I took games by the scruff of the neck, now I was just happy to play a part, get it and pass it and just drift through matches. I was doing enough and no more. I couldn't see myself dictating a game when there were so many people around who had won a championship. I just lacked self-confidence. I was happy to be there, but not justifying my place. Peter was dominating the game but having a sticky patch and some of the fans turned against him. I will always remember how he never hid and always wanted the ball. It was something I learned from him. No matter how badly he was playing he would still try and lift the players around him. It was a great characteristic that I tried to copy. Looking back I never gave him the support he needed. It was my fault, I never rose to it, I was in my own little shell.

I don't have many regrets in life, but one is that it took so long to show Everton supporters what I was made of. They must have wondered why they had paid so much for someone who was all right but nothing more. Maybe if my dad had gone to games and pointed things out it would have been better. Some of my old Bradford mates said I lacked confidence, so it was obvious to everyone.

When Reidy went we got even worse. We lost four and drew three and the pressure was mounting. There was only the FA Cup to keep us going. We were getting by at tough places like West Brom and Plymouth and won at Barnsley. I even got the Player of the Month award at the club for February. I sat down and decided it was time to get my finger out. Colin never said much to me, but I wanted to repay him fast. He was looking for a blend all over the park but wasn't getting one. The new lads were toiling. Neil was dropped after a month, Pat was injured and Tony was inconsistent.

The Wimbledon quarter-final was a huge game for the club and me, or so I thought. They were the holders, it was live on TV and I scored the winner. Then came a sledgehammer blow just a few days later. On a shocking night in Newcastle we went down 2–0. I missed a great chance and I was taken off. It was impossible to play that night and I didn't think too much more about it. On the Saturday morning my dad rang and said what's this in the paper about me being dropped. I laughed and asked where he got that news from. He said it was on the back pages. I went out and got them and saw the headline screaming '£3 million axe – Cottee and McCall to be dropped'. I rang my dad back and said it was just paper talk as nothing had been said to me. I was certain Colin would have told me first and even after seeing the news I didn't believe it. I thought I was playing reasonably well, but when I reached the ground it was obvious that the press were right. I saw Colin after the game, very disappointed, not about being dropped but because the newspapers knew before me. Colin assured me that they had just taken a lucky guess. He said he was really disappointed about the Newcastle game and could have left any one of seven of us out. He felt it was my turn.

Being axed was a blessing in the end. It gave me a chance to look at the games and see for myself what to do next time I was in. I saw I could do all that, but hadn't been. Colin wanted me to be more commanding, be what I was at Bradford, get a grip. I wasn't doing that but I realised I could. I had also been putting myself under pressure before by thinking I could be dropped, but that had been lifted as well.

I was only on the bench for the semi-final with Norwich. That was the day of the Hillsborough disaster. News filtered through to the dressing-room quickly and no one was celebrating. I drove back that night to Leeds and stopped off near Birmingham for a bite to eat. The local papers had pictures of the crush and these faces on the front page. I was shocked. I wondered how the families would feel who might see their loved ones like that. There were so many Everton fans who had Liverpool fans as relatives or friends and I just hoped none would see anyone they knew in those pictures. It was like Bradford again. I kept the radio on and the death toll kept rising. The whole awful day touched everyone, not just red but also blue. Britain was in mourning, but nowhere more than Merseyside. Football seemed irrelevant as grief and sadness sank in.

Fortunately Liverpool made the final and set up a great day for football. The build-up for me was mixed. I was in and out of the side, but it was pretty obvious that the midfield four would be Pat and Kevin on the wings with Trevor Steven and Brace in the middle. I had some good games as we won at Manchester United and beat Derby, but even then I was just waiting for the next season to start rather than thinking too much about the final. I knew now what I had to do, I felt better in myself. It was a mental thing all along and my mind was right for a fresh start rather than Wembley.

The whole of the country, apart from Evertonians, wanted Liverpool to win. The scramble for a place on the bench was huge. Pat van den Hauwe, our tough left-back, was carrying an injury so Neil Pointon might have been needed to take his place. So it was between him, Ian Wilson, Wayne Clarke and myself for the two slots. I thought Wayne would be one because Colin would go for a striker. The Thursday and Friday were very tense for us all. It wasn't until Saturday lunchtime, around 12.30, that I got the nod and even then maybe by accident. After our pre-match meal I was going up the stairs to the second floor. Colin by chance was behind me. It was the longest walk ever. I could hear his footsteps behind and was waiting for him to say something like 'I'm leaving you out'. I was just going into the corridor towards my room when he said: 'You're sub today, Macca.' I felt so relieved all I could blurt out was: 'I won't let you down today, boss.' It sounds corny, but it's all I could come out with. I rang my mum and dad to tell them. They hadn't even come down to the game although my brother Les, brother-in-law Alan and close pal Paul were at

Wembley. On the way to the match it became obvious that Colin had not told the other three lads what the decision was. I used my discretion and kept it to myself. It was only in the dressing-room that he told Ian Wilson he was the other. So much for my guess about Neil Pointon and Wayne Clarke.

The next thing was to get on at Wembley. It was a 90-degree heat and on that turf there is always the chance that someone will get tired, so I was optimistic of a run. I came on around the hour for Bracewell. Liverpool were leading 1–0 through John Aldridge and were dictating the game. We had taken a bit of a chasing and Brace had run himself into the ground. I really enjoyed it because we got on top for the first time in the last ten minutes. Dave Watson was pushed up and hit a shot that was parried by Bruce Grobbelaar. I've always been deadly from a yard and managed to toe it in. But I still didn't know if I had scored. I had just stretched out and made contact, I couldn't see anything. I spotted Tony Cottee running away and celebrating and I thought he had got it. I asked him and he said: 'No, you scored.' It was only later I found out he was in the back of the net and technically offside.

It was a great lift for us to equalise so late and just before extra-time. We were encouraged to go at them. They were looking drained. They had their hands on the trophy and we had snatched it back. I believed we were the only side who would win it, but I counted without their sub Ian Rush. As always he scored – he seemed to in all the derby games. But then came my moment of history. Alan Hansen headed the ball out, I chested it down, volleyed it for the corner and saw it go in past Grobbelaar's fingertips. It was the first time a sub had scored twice in an FA Cup final, but unfortunately Rushy repeated the feat a couple of minutes later. If we had held on for a few minutes more I am sure we would have won.

There was plenty of disappointment at the final whistle, but I remember the fans came on because the fences were down and some were coming up and saying not to mind there was next season. The Everton supporters seemed cheerful and it was good to know we had not let them down too badly. The invasion spoiled it for Liverpool – they couldn't do a lap of honour – but it was a fitting tribute to them and their fans that they had won the Cup. If it had been 1–0 it would have been a dull day, but it turned out one of the best finals ever. We'd made it a game to remember although defeat was still hard to stomach.

Days later we went to Magalluf for a break and it was just as well as Liverpool were going for the double that week with a final league game against Arsenal. We had been out in the sun for most of the day and had a few beers early on. We found a pub with a TV and gathered to watch the inevitable. Arsenal had to do the impossible and win 2–0. When you live in the same city as a team that's done the double it must be hard. It puts you under more pressure from your fans and the criticism gets worse because you are being compared unfavourably with them. For that reason we were hoping the Gunners did it. Alan Smith scored for Arsenal, but time was running out and Steve McMahon was signalling one minute left to his mates. We were drinking up, ready to go home in disappointment when all hell broke loose. Michael Thomas scored the second. From going home early the lads all went out till the small hours to toast the result. It's crazy, but that's football. Thanks to that result it made our poor season easier to take for us and the fans. It's not being cynical, it's just human nature. It was just like that time when John Brown and the Dundee boys were happy United lost in Europe. Now I understood.

The summer saw Colin make some more signings and you felt it was his team now. Norman Whiteside arrived from Manchester United, Stefan Rehn from Sweden, Ray Atteveld from Holland and Mike Newell and Martin Keown were also big-name captures. There were not many of the old guard left – Trevor Steven and Wayne Clarke moved out. With Norman coming to play in midfield I could have been worried, but I heard that Colin had turned down interest from Leeds in me and I was delighted. I wanted to give this a go and the chance to play with Big Norm was exciting. We were in the middle together from the start in pre-season and we beat his old club United in Japan. I was impressed straightaway with the ability of the big lad. He was also such a nice guy off the park and in my book he was a great signing for the year or so he lasted.

The togetherness in pre-season was good, although I had a bit of a discussion with Kevin Ratcliffe about football and what had gone wrong the season before. It got a bit heated, but I didn't think much of it at the time. Tony Cottee came over and Ratters made a remark like 'What are your plans for next season?' to him and that stuck in my mind. It was disparaging to him and unnecessary.

The season started well and although we lost at Coventry we won our next two and I managed to break my league duck against Southampton. Then we beat Manchester United 3–2 in a tremendous game before winning at Charlton to go top of the league. We came back to earth when Liverpool beat us in the derby, but I was pleased with our form and got a Scotland under-21 call-up as an average player against France. It was a relief as I had been out of the international picture for 18 months or so. I was captain and Craig Brown pulled me afterwards and told me to keep up the good work because there would be a chance in the big team down the line. I roomed with a young lad called Eoin Jess who came on for the last 20 minutes but I thought immediately that he had the makings of a top player. He is still to fulfil that promise totally, but he has won a few caps nonetheless.

Club and country were going hand in hand. Andy Roxburgh came down to see us beat Luton 3–0 and I was tipped to make the squad for the final qualifier with Norway. Colin Harvey said I was the most consistent player in the team, although privately he said I should be scoring more goals which was fair comment. I made the Norway squad and it was a big night as Scotland got through. I was in the stand but I still got a taste and wanted to be involved as soon as possible. Andy told me it was up to myself to force him to pick me with my club performances. The World Cup in Italy was more a dream than reality to me.

Everton's form took a major slump when we were thumped 6–2 at Aston Villa, a game where Peter Beagrie made his debut as a sub. The team was not gelling on or off the park.

Naturally when things go wrong people point the finger at others and this was beginning to happen at Everton. There was an uneasy atmosphere between a couple of the senior players and the new boys. Just before Christmas Colin took us to Marbella for a golf break and to help team spirit. He must have been feeling it himself. But it poured non-stop and we spent most of our time in the hotel bar. I have learned down the years that football talk and drink don't mix. People begin to say what they really feel and that was the case here. Tony Cottee had a heated argument with Kevin Sheedy about football – he thought Sheeds only crossed to Sharpy instead of him. Although things were said I thought it had all been forgotten when we got home, but the bad feelings were becoming a strong undercurrent.

At the club Christmas party it reared its ugly head again. Well into the night I was in a row with Kevin Ratcliffe's brother. He was making the point that the decline in Everton's fortunes had started with the arrival of the new players. He said Tony Cottee would never be another Andy Gray and that I was no Peter Reid. That was all true in its way, Tony was as different to Andy as I was to Peter. Both of them had lifted Everton under Howard Kendall when his job was on the line. It was through their spirit and enthusiasm that the club had risen. Ratcliffe's brother also went on about the new boys not performing since they joined, which again I could only agree with. But I told him that the players who had won the championship were not doing the business at that level or anywhere near it either.

What annoyed me was that Ratcliffe's brother mentioned one or two things that had been secret within the dressing-room and could only have come from Kevin. It dawned on me that what he was saying was really what Kevin thought and not his opinions. He was saying what Kevin was thinking. The trouble was that both sides of the argument were right, both 'camps' were not doing that well and that was causing the friction.

One of the major accusations was that the new boys never mixed with the rest off the park. Again there was something in that. It was something I had believed in at Bradford where it was one out, all out. The reasons for that at Everton were that a lot of the lads lived in Southport and most would head out for a few beers after the games. Neil McDonald, who was a friend and my room-mate, took the most stick for being miserable and not going out. But he had a young family and had a few problems with the health of his child. Tony Cottee was also a family man and after being away he didn't like leaving his young family on their own. I could see both points of view and at times I got stuck in the middle of this dispute. In fact it earned me the name Cinderella. I would go out for a few and then be back by midnight. The lads slaughtered me for going early and then the wife had a go and asked why I was back later than Neil and Tony. Sometimes you can't win.

When we went out it was great, but there were divisions caused by the results. It's difficult when you have a successful team and then they lose that magic. It's easy to blame the new boys for the change. It was an underlying problem. You could tell people were talking behind backs all the time, it would go quiet in a dressing-room when you went into it. It's a problem I had never known before and I found it all very disappointing. I think we would have done a lot better as a team if everyone had got on better. I am sure Colin realised deep down what was happening but could not do anything to change it. He could not force people out to socialise with each other. It sounds trivial but it's an important aspect of any club.

Ratters was the captain but he did a fair bit of mixing. He was outside that argument about socialising with the school in Southport, yet he was always stirring it up. That became obvious from the argument with his brother. When he said I would never be a Peter Reid I wondered if that was Kevin's view. It just simmered with me after that. Maybe it's no coincidence that Neville Southall and Dave Watson were the star men that season. They were outside that little argument.

That Christmas trouble must have fired me up because on Boxing Day I scored a 25-yarder past Peter Shilton to beat Derby 1–0. I had played in 37 out of 38 league games that season and made my debut for Scotland against Argentina.

From a personal point of view it was a good one – the team were third until the last three games but ended up sixth. It was an improvement but still not good enough. Neville got the two main Player of the Year awards and was truly outstanding and I was chuffed to get the vote as the best outfield player just ahead of Norman. He had a great start and although he couldn't get up and down any more he was a real threat when he got in the box. His passing and control were excellent, you could not get near him. The only trouble was his injury problems. It was such a shame that he only managed the one full season with us. His career was sadly cut short. If he had been fit for longer so many things could have turned out differently.

Chapter 8

Ups and downs of Italia 90

It's hard to believe that I didn't get my Scotland call until March 1990 with just a matter of weeks to the World Cup finals. Everything happened so fast, not just for me but also the other lads who came in on an experimental night that will always live with me. We must have been struggling for midfield players at the time. There were three of us who came in, Craig Levein, Robert Fleck and me, while Stewart McKimmie was only getting his second cap and Gary McAllister was soon to be in the squad. It was all change after the qualifying match the November before and when I made the squad against Argentina I didn't expect to play never mind make the World Cup. I was hoping for a decent game just to get a call-up in the future. I never imagined I was going to be an ever-present from then on until the finals. I think it is the quickest first eight caps that have ever been awarded.

I had only been in the under-21s a few times and Andy Roxburgh must have taken that into account, but I still think if I had had a shocker against Argentina that could have been it, a one-cap wonder. To represent your country is huge, to start against the World Cup holders is even bigger. All the build-up was about whether Maradona would come – he didn't come, he must have heard I was playing! It also helped that three of us were starting together. The focus was not just on me. Roxy just told me to do what I did for Everton. They just wanted enthusiasm and that I could guarantee. I was just to get the ball for Paul McStay and Jim Bett. I was up against this boy Batista who was a monster, a gorilla with a beard. He was scary to look at but as the game went on I wasn't frightened any more. To cap my debut I set up Stewart McKimmie for the winner. We had beaten the World Cup holders, a side who would get to the final again soon after.

It didn't sink in until I was driving back to Merseyside. It was only then that I realised what had happened. I had fulfilled that dream every Scot has. I had played for Scotland, I had played at Hampden, one of the last times it was full. From my earliest days it was all I wanted to do. My mind went back to the days when I went to Wembley to be part of the Tartan Army, like the time in 1981 when John Robertson scored the only goal with a penalty. We were banned from getting tickets, but my pal Paul and I made it. I had left early on the Saturday, about 6 a.m., with just a Scotland scarf. At every service station on the way down I stopped and got another piece of tartan memorabilia. By the time I got to Wembley I had the scarf, a tartan bunnet, a flag and a banner round my neck. I won't forget walking up Wembley Way with 70,000 Scots singing 'We beat the ticket ban' at the top of our voices. Straight after the game we got a bus back to Leeds and I was in the pub for the highlights, dressed in tartan. The barman asked if I had been watching it in the house – it was only when I brought out the programme he believed I had been there. To think I had actually played in front of those fans gave me one of the biggest highs of my life.

I stayed in the side for the next few warm-up matches and I thought it was looking good for the finals. Every game brought them nearer. The results were not too clever but I was getting good vibes from the management. I was in the squad and soon realised I was probably going to start. We had a trip to Malta before the finals and it was an idea of Andy's to split us up in groups and go out to different restaurants. I was out with Gary Mac, a shy fellow called Ally McCoist, Jim Bett, the great Davie Cooper and Murdo McLeod. I was shocked when

Coops and Jazzer pulled me aside and asked me what school I went to. I didn't know what they were on about. What team did I support up in Scotland? I told them Rangers and I was surprised to find out Murdo, although an ex-Celt, was also a Rangers fan. It was a bit of fun but Coops proudly announced as we sat down that we were all in good Rangers company . . . Craig Brown too.

I never really knew the great Davie Cooper well before that trip, but he made me very welcome, he helped me settle and made me feel relaxed. I still had this English accent and felt a bit of an outsider, but thankfully Andy Goram was in the squad and his accent was as bad as mine. We won that Malta game 2–1 thanks to a couple from big Rambo, Alan McInally, and I thought I had done enough to make the World Cup opener with Costa Rica. Although the build-up results were poor, with no one giving us a chance of making the second stage in the finals in Italy, we had a sense of determination within the squad. At least with Costa Rica first we could get off to a flier.

The game kicked off late afternoon and the sun was beating down. Before the game Andy Roxburgh had said their keeper was dodgy on crosses and we should put him under pressure. That was why big Nally got in ahead of Coisty, who was so disappointed after teaming up with Mo Johnston in so many games before. Of course the keeper caught every ball we threw into the box and made a mockery of the assessments we had been given. We still had loads of chances, but they scored from one of their few. I still thought we would get back into it, but I was now living the old horrors of past years like Peru and Iran in 1978. The dressing-room afterwards was just a scene of devastation.We were totally humiliated. We had let the country down and knew it. No fingers were pointed, it wasn't a shocking performance, just a shocking result. There was only one way to repay those fans – beat Sweden.

To make things worse we had the incident with wee Mo and Jim Bett who were set up and pictured out drinking with fans. They were just in a quiet bar causing no one any harm. It got blown up out of all proportion, but in a way all the stick brought us together and made us even stronger as a unit.

There were quite a few changes – there had to be. I was just relieved to get a second chance, on my birthday too. I was surprised the two experienced boys in midfield, McStay and Bett, were chopped. It was a brave decision and Roxy also brought in Robert Fleck beside Mo. He had seen Flecky give Glenn Hysen, the Swedish skipper, a hard time in a club game and thought he could trouble him again. We also had Gordon Durie back down the left and the fans were still with us. Before the game I saw the flags and they looked equal in numbers, but the noise from the Tartan Army was five times louder than the Swedes as we took over Genoa.

It was also a bit loud in the tunnel. I have never known a team so psyched up before a match. It was not about tactics, just determination. This was going to be a British Cup tie and one we would win. Big Roy Aitken, Alex McLeish and even Flecky were growling and shouting at the Swedes. 'Come on,' 'Get intae them,' just pure Scottish passion. We could hear the fans too and although the Swedes had some giants they looked shocked. It was on that high that we started and could not have carried on any better.

The plan was for me to sit at the edge of the box if we won a corner. Davie McPherson was supposed to win the header at the near post and knock it on for wee Mo to shoot. Sure enough Gordon Durie picked out big Slim McPherson and from where I was, where I was supposed to stay, I just gambled and got in front of Mo and poked the ball in from three yards out. It is probably the proudest moment of my career . . . and my only goal for Scotland.

The game was just a battle and late on big Roy did his dying swan act and won a penalty. Mo stuck it away and although the Swedes got one back it was a result to make you feel great to be a Scot. It was eight years since we had won a major match at the World Cup finals and it's arguably the biggest result we have ever had at that stage. The fans certainly felt that way and I will never forget how they draped themselves round the bus afterwards and would not let us move. We had shared their pain against Costa Rica and now had the widest grins in the whole of Italy. We had a meal and a few beers later and I whiled away the hours playing cards – there was no chance of sleeping. It didn't even matter that I lost most of my win bonus to Juke Box Durie at cards. So what?

We went to Turin needing a point against Brazil to qualify for the second round for the first time ever. They only needed one point as well and I don't know how we lost that one. Jim Leighton only had one save to make and although they had stars like Romario, Careca and Dunga, whom I was up against, they always looked as though they were in second gear. History was about to be written when they scored with eight minutes left through the big boy Muller, but we should still have got a draw. With seconds to go I found Flecky whose shot deflected to Mo and his shot was miraculously saved by Taffarel. I think it was voted save of the tournament later, but that was no consolation. It was the same old story for us and we had to wait another day to find out if results would go our way and save us.

I never even watched the other matches. I knew we were out, it was just the way. Uruguay scored in injury-time to get the result they needed and then it was down to Holland and the Republic of Ireland. If they drew they both made it, so of course they did. It just seemed inevitable to me that it wasn't to be. I felt we were out after the Brazil game. The disappointment of packing your bags and heading home was hard to take.

I reflected that it had been enjoyable to have played in the best competition against some of the best players just four months after making my debut. It was the start of a new Scotland side with people like Gary McAllister and John Collins coming through. Gary and I got close as we roomed together and I had the distraction of teaching him all the Leeds songs because he had just joined them from Leicester. I wanted more of this in a hurry. One extra thing I took home from Italy was a Seiko watch for scoring the sixth fastest goal of the tournament. It was some consolation, but I was still empty at coming so close and yet so far.

Chapter 9

Howard's way

I came back from the World Cup and signed a new deal with Everton. It was all thanks to Tony Cottee because when he came to the club all the other boys went in for rises as he was on so much and the word got round. I got the call to get an increase and was content enough to sign it. I was happy. I had won international recognition with Everton and was willing to commit my peak years to them. Just to make things even better we had moved into a new house in Formby and my little lad Lee was born in August. It was all systems go.

The boss had signed Andy Hinchcliffe and Mike Milligan, but we got off to a disastrous start. We lost the first game at home to Leeds in a match made famous by Neville Southall's sit-down strike. He just sat in the goalmouth while the rest of us had our dressing-room talk at half-time. I always got on well with Nev, he gave out stick no matter who you were, he didn't care. No one ever talked back because he was just too big. He was rough and ready and a total one-off. He never touched a drink, which also made him different. He never mixed with the boys, just went home to his family in Llandudno. Pre-match meals for Nev were bacon and egg, never mind this pasta nonsense. Nev said what he thought and bugger the consequences. He was a real pro and I respected his dedication. I still don't know why he did it, but

I think it was personal. I believe he felt it more than anyone when Everton were on the slide. I think he was fed up with himself as well as the team and those frustrations made him sit alone.

I was having trouble with injuries and could not do much to help as the team faltered, although I scored in the Merseyside derby – we still lost 3–2. You could tell the tension was getting to Colin. He was first and foremost an Everton supporter. He felt for them as much as for himself I could see how desperate he was to give them something. This was his team and it was not happening. Colin was very intense, he felt let down by a lot of his players although I can't recall him having a go at them publicly. I could see it getting to him as the pressure from the media and the fans mounted.

Colin had an idea to lift the spirits by taking us out for a Chinese meal. It was an old Everton tradition and was a bonding exercise, so it sounded worth a try. This was the first time most of the new boys had been for a Chinese, but there was a good turn-out as we wanted things to improve for everybody's good. Early on it was good-humoured, but again drink was the winner. That was when the trouble started. The talk had been of getting better and was light stuff for a while but then it turned personal. About 11 at night Mike Milligan, Dave Watson and myself joined Sheeds, Martin Keown and Ray Atteveld at a big pub, the Carlton, and by that time everyone was the worse for wear. Martin didn't drink much and the topic came round to his ability. Sheeds can be quite sharp-tongued in drink and he was telling Martin what he thought of him. Kevin was an artistic player with a super left foot and plenty of technique, while Martin was a 110 per center and physical. They both felt the other should have more of the qualities they had as that was what the team was lacking.

Martin thought we should fight more, while Sheeds said we needed more ability. Dave Watson and I told him to cut it out as Martin wasn't in the mood because he wasn't drinking, but Sheeds was pretty serious. The final insult was when he said Martin couldn't trap a bag of cement. That was it. Martin rained a few blows on Sheeds. He rolled into a ball trying to protect himself but still kept shouting out his jibes at big Martin. Dave and I tried our best to pull him off, but Martin had lost it a bit. Sheeds needed four stitches in his eye.

Colin heard about the trouble and brought them together to make up. I don't think Sheeds remembered too much about it, but the trouble was down to frustration. Sheeds was disappointed to be out of the team, while Martin was out of the side too. He never really settled and he and Ratcliffe were not on the same wavelength either. The Keown-Sheedy affair was a clash of personalities but it was also a part of the old boy-new boy split that was still below the surface and spilled over occasionally. If things had been going well they would never have had that fall-out, they would have been slapping each other on the back. Poor Colin had arranged the Chinese to bring in harmony among the lads and it ended in a scuffle in a pub.

On 30 October Colin got the sack. You could see it coming. We were in the bottom three and the last straw was losing to Sheffield United in the League Cup. It was a sad day for me – Colin brought me to the club and gave me a new stage. He worked tremendously hard, his training was good and he was fully committed to bringing success to the club. I rang him and offered my best wishes as well as my apologies. When a boss is sacked you ask yourself what you could have done and I felt I had let him down.

Jimmy Gabriel took over as temporary boss and I was hoping Joe Royle would get the job. He had always been complimentary towards me and I would have recommended him straightaway. But I was sitting outside Tesco's in Southport when I caught the end of the news and heard them say they would have more on the sensational new Everton appointment on their next bulletin. It couldn't be Royle as that would have been no great surprise. A lad rapped on my car window and asked if I had heard the great news that Howard Kendall is back. My chin hit the floor and was quickly followed by my heart. I had seen what he did at Manchester City by bringing in all his old mates like Alan Harper, Adrian

Heath and Reidy and I thought he would probably favour all of his pals at the club when he came. That was the last thing I thought we needed, more division in the ranks.

Instead my first impressions when Howard came were of his enthusiasm and his new ideas in training. He also brought Colin back as number two. We worked a lot more on possession and he brought in little drills in training that lifted things. I was also happy Colin was back in work both for him and me. The alternative was Reidy and I thought if he came that could be the end of me. Things went okay and I scored in a live televised drawn match with Spurs and despite a couple of defeats I got the winner against Coventry. We were on the up again.

One of the other tricks Howard brought in was the introduction of bottles of wine at meal times, even the night before a game. This was something he had done before and also a habit they were into during his time in Spain. The majority had the odd glass, but one time some of the boys had more than a few because they thought they weren't going to be playing the next day. It was the night before the ZDS final at Wembley against Crystal Palace and no one was taking it too seriously. Some of them were shocked when Howard sprang a surprise and named them to play at Wembley. Needless to say we lost the game 4–1. The same thing happened before a match at Leeds when two lads on the fringe of the squad got quite merry and were shocked to be picked the next day, playing with serious hangovers.

There was often a drink about when you least expected it. I picked up a cup in the dressing-room before a game and thought it was half full of Lucozade. I took a swig and had to spit it out. It was whisky and I didn't touch that since the 'Hear, hear, Lawrie' incident. I don't know who it belonged to, but it wasn't there when they got back.

Kendall's Everton were winning again and I never got left out once, which was a surprise as I had feared the worst when he arrived. He chopped and changed, but he was fair-minded. Some of the older lads like Sharpy and Sheeds were also dropped so there was no old pals act about. There was also the

FA Cup to look forward to and we drew Liverpool in the fifth round to set up three memorable games and a bust-up with the boss.

We held them 0–0 at Anfield and I was part of a defensive formation that was effective. I was under orders to stop John Barnes from playing and I thought it worked. The replay was three days later and I knew we would be more attacking and was dying to get involved in that. We went away to a hotel in Haydock and about 5 p.m. the boss pulled me just before our team meeting. He said we were going to be more offensive at home and I said great, let's get at them. I had never been on the winning side against Liverpool in my previous eight derbies and thought this was going to be the one. I was up and confident and raring to go. I was thinking he had pulled me to say I was to keep an eye on Barnes or to stay tight to Jan Molby, but instead he finished his sentence: 'Mike Newell's coming back and you are the one to be left out!' I just flipped. I was amazed and then stunned and almost immediately angry. I lashed out at the first thing near me and booted the fire door good and hard. It shot open and there was an almighty noise. I was so shocked, not that I thought I was too big to be dropped, just at the timing of it, just a couple of hours before a game I was really pumped up for. I had tears of anger in my eyes as he told me to get along to the meeting-room. As he went through the team at the back of the room I was in a trance. It was only when he named the subs and asked if I was up to being one that I came round from my daze and nodded.

It was amazing as those were the only 45 minutes when I wasn't in his team. I came on at half-time. The first half went badly as we tried a system of Sharpy and Mike Newell up front with Pat Nevin behind them. Liverpool were strong down their left so everything came down that flank and poor Ray Atteveld was swamped at right-back. We went one down and it could have been four. To Kendall's credit he changed it at the break. Pat went wide, Neil Mac to right-back and we had more balance. Nobody could have guessed that was to turn into the best derby game seen with me coming on and, more significantly, TC with under ten minutes to go. Rushy had done the usual and put them 3–2 up but with seconds left I got a touch through to Tony who equalised. John Barnes scored a cracker in extra-time but Tony took it to a third game. Two days later came the staggering news that Kenny Dalglish had resigned. There was no sign of pressure getting to him during the game and I often wonder if he would have gone if they had held on 3–2 or 4–3.

That was one of Tony's finest hours and I feel sorry for him as he never got the praise he deserved for his goals. Like me with Reidy his partnership with Graeme Sharp, which he wanted to succeed, never really worked. I don't think they ever got the best service, although if you gave Tony a chance he would usually score. Tony was given a lot of criticism for being lazy, but it was never his style to go charging about the pitch. Yet when he left his scoring record would compare favourably with most.

I had never reacted before as I did when I was dropped that night and I was frankly embarrassed about it afterwards. The third game against Liverpool finally brought revenge over them, thanks to Dave Watson's goal. I enjoyed those games against McMahon and Ronnie Whelan and I thought there was very little between us apart from Rush's goals. They also had world-class talent in Barnes and Peter Beardsley. We never really had a matchwinner like that and that was the difference. This time we did it, and with West Ham in the quarters, Wembley was a possibility.

Unfortunately Stuart Slater had the game of his life and we went out, our season over. We finished ninth on the back of a six-game unbeaten run, which was quite an achievement considering the mess we were in when Kendall took over. Sometimes he did things that didn't work out, but he was a gambler. No one could feel complacent with him around. He was also a man for a wind-up, as I found out on another time when he left me speechless.

We went on a break in January and the newspapers had me joining Rangers. The lads were on about it non-stop, revving me up to ask the boss about it and Howard heard. He called me over and asked if I had anything to say to him. If I wanted to go to Rangers he would just call up Graeme Souness. I thought it was all in jest. I forgot all about it, but when we got back he called me into the office. The phone was in his hand and he said: 'Stuart, I've got Graeme Souness on the line, would you like a word?' I went bright red and ran out of his room. I was amazed that he had remembered.

Kendall would always enjoy a craic with the lads on those trips. He knew the right time to do it, but he had some memory even when you thought he couldn't be taking things in. Even when you thought he was out of it he was aware of all that was going on. Maybe we would not have had that Chinese problem if he had been with us. He was the type who could handle situations like that personally and probably be the last man standing. The atmosphere under Howard got better.

The next season, 1991–92, started with talk that Howard wanted to buy. Peter Beardsley was his big target, but the club were short of cash so some might have to go. I was thrilled when he got Beardsley and he joined us in Switzerland for a pre-season tour. We played four games in ten days and I was beside him in midfield and really anticipating a good partnership in the months ahead. I thought he was a great signing and he proved to be.

Unknown to Everton I was contacted by a journalist and asked if I would be keen to join Rangers. There was a move on to sell Trevor Steven to Marseille but even before I could consider my answer that fell through. I thought nothing of it and then Walter Smith rang me. I had never spoken to him before, but he was persuasive and said that he wanted me if the Steven deal went ahead. I wasn't looking to leave Everton, in fact I was pretty settled, so my mind was in turmoil. I knew Howard had too many midfielders and would have to sell but the days passed and nothing happened.

The Tuesday before the season began in England we flew to Spain to play Real Sociedad and the writing was suddenly on the wall. I was just sub and I read the script fast. It was me who was going. The European deadline was that Thursday, so the Rangers move would have to happen soon or not at all. But with those thoughts racing round my mind there was a welcome distraction in the shape of my last night out with the boys of Everton.

While we were out Evel Knievel, sometimes known as Peter Beagrie, had managed to get hold of a moped. This was after he had got a hold of a few beers previously and the pair did not blend. He had come back to the hotel after a tour of the city, couldn't find the boys and decided he wanted to park his vehicle in the hotel foyer, which was up a flight of steps and through a revolving door. Now Peter thought it would be an idea to take the bike up the steps while he was still sitting on it. He took off, went too fast and crashed straight through the window and into the headlines. His arm needed over 60 stitches.

When we got home I got a call to say the Rangers move was still possible. I had told the lads on the trip, but still expected to be with them against Nottingham Forest on the Saturday. I didn't really grasp just how quickly I had to move to Rangers.

In fact it was only a stroke of luck and bending the rules a bit that made the Rangers deal happen. By chance I was due to go to a barbecue at Neil McDonald's house on the Thursday, but because it was pouring we stayed at home. The phone goes and it's my agent saying if I want to sign for Rangers I will have to get the 7 p.m. flight from Manchester. The only snag was that Everton didn't know yet that Rangers were in for me or had agreed a price, so really it was an illegal approach and all cloak-and-dagger stuff. Fortunately Neil finally got through. We met up at the airport and I had to pretend it was all news to me when Everton telephoned to ask me if I fancied the idea. I tried to play dumb, but it didn't work. They asked if I could make the airport quickly to get to Edinburgh for talks. I said I would try, but then they heard the announcements for passengers to board in the background. I think Everton sussed I was already at Manchester airport. I imagine the call for the Edinburgh flight gave it away.

Although Rangers had been in my heart as a boy it was still a major upheaval to go to Scotland. It was only after a brief conversation with Howard, who told me honestly and openly that he needed money for other players, that I knew I had to go. He made my mind up for me in Manchester airport with the minutes ticking away. I knew Walter Smith was keen to sign me and that Kendall would let me go. It was a simple equation in the end.

We met Archie Knox and he took us to see the chairman, David Murray, in his offices. About 9.30 p.m. it was all agreed and I just had to get through to Glasgow for a quick medical to tie it all up by the midnight deadline for Europe. What I didn't know was that Trevor Steven was being sold to Marseille officials who were in the next room, thrashing out their details with Mr Murray. The chairman took great delight in telling me that later on and reminding me that if I had played hard to get he would have given Everton £1.5 million instead of £1.2 million and I would also have had more money crammed in my pockets to sign in time. He was just about to bank £5 million and I could have asked for a few more quid. I found out quickly what a shrewd operator he is.

Finance wasn't the issue. I was increasing my wages, but I was joining one of the biggest clubs in Europe. I had taken a lot of time thinking about the decision – moving the family from Southport was a big deal – but Howard Kendall made it easy in the end. It turned out to be the best thing that happened, so thanks, Howard.

I had a good relationship with Everton's fans and made many friends. I enjoyed those last two seasons but let myself down in the first one. I played 11 times for Scotland while I was there, something I would probably never have done at Bradford. I got some nice mail when I left. It's ironic that they did eventually bring in Joe Royle as boss and went on to win the FA Cup. These things are all about timing and who knows the way it would have worked if Joe had come, and not Howard, back then? However, my time with him was nowhere near as bad as I thought it would be and the only drawbacks were not getting to play more with Beardsley and not impressing the fans that bit quicker.

Chapter 10

Taking the high road

Everything happened so quickly when I signed for Rangers that I didn't meet the lads until Friday, just a day before my debut at Hearts. It was a help that I knew so many from the Scotland squads, but I was still out of breath. The pre-season has been stop-start for me and I had heard the Scottish game was quicker, so I was a bit unsure before the first game. I was also concerned that people would see me as a replacement for Trevor Steven. I wasn't, we were two totally different players – for a start he could play! I had time to take a look round Ibrox and realised why I was there. The stadium was superb, although it's got even better since. I knew I had made the right decision.

There was plenty happening at the time with Walter Smith just taking over from Graeme Souness and making some heavy spending in the transfer market. He signed Andy Goram, Davie Robertson and also Alexei Mikhailechenko. My debut went well . . . for about 30 seconds. Scott Crabbe hit a long-range shot that Andy misjudged and that was the winner. I got booked before half-time, so it was a bad day all round. I found out at half-time about the levels Walter would demand. He let us know that the standards the club had set must be maintained and we had to carry on being successful. In no uncertain terms he told the defenders and captain Richard

Gough in particular that he was not happy with them. They were playing it around at the back and not hurting Hearts. He wanted them to get it forward quicker for Mo Johnston and Mark Hateley. It came as a shock to me. If we had played like that at Everton we would have felt it was something to build on. At Rangers you were expected to win every week, home or away, to be classed as successful.

My first game at Ibrox was a Skol Cup tie with Queens Park, which again showed me the difference between Everton and Rangers. If that had been Goodison for a game against Rochdale, for example, we might have got just over 10,000. There were 32,000 at Ibrox. We won 6–0 and Mo scored four.

The first taste of the Old Firm games was an even bigger jolt to the system. We were staying in a city centre hotel and it was as if everybody was either blue or green. The demand for tickets was unbelievable. The place was in turmoil and everyone was on one side or another. I used to get a taxi to training from the hotel, which cost two or three quid normally, but that week if you got a Celtic fan driving it was a tenner and if it was a Rangers fan you got a freebie. Or you could go to McDonald's and either get extra McNuggets or just half a bag of chips. It was intense everywhere you went. I couldn't even get away from it in a cake shop where a lady of about 70 recognised me and told me we had to win as it would make her husband's day, her son's day and also her grandson's day. I had come from Merseyside, where it was a friendly rivalry, to the most fierce split in Britain.

I was living in the city centre and the passion and hatred was in the air. You could feel it. No one had prepared me for it, you had to be in Glasgow to appreciate it. The foreign lads down the years must wonder what they have walked into. It is quite frightening. In general most of the boys live outside the centre of Glasgow and in fairness enjoy living in the area and the friendliness of the people. It's just when the Old Firm games come along that you have to be careful where you go out and about in the city. I was staying slap bang in the middle and the days heading up to the game were very intense. The first one was at Parkhead where I was against Gary Gillespie, who had the upper hand from Mersey derby games with Liverpool. But I set up big Mark for the first goal and we won 2–0. It was just a wall of noise. You could tell how much it meant that week with people congratulating you for days afterwards. I was in the hotel with two kids and a dog and every time you went out of the door people were talking football. It was claustrophobic and I was stuck there for six months because we could not sell the house in Southport.

We drew Sparta Prague in the first round of the European Cup and my first experience of that level. We lost 1–0 in Prague but I had only seen Scottish games on TV and so I was more roused by the thought of playing the home tie because I had watched the excitement in those games before and wanted some myself. Before that return leg we had two disasters in a row, losing to Hibs in the Skol Cup semi and then being beaten by our big rivals, Aberdeen, in the league at Ibrox.

The Sparta game went well for me personally, but was a sickener for the club. I scored one to take the tie into extra-time. I even managed a second, but a mix-up between Andy Goram and Scott Nisbet cost us an away goal and we were out. The alarm bells were ringing. The boss was getting stick and he was only two months into the season. The bad run was being put down to his signings – I was unscathed but Andy was getting most criticism. He had a sticky start but has more than made up for that down the years and has been an absolutely outstanding keeper for club and country.

The big change was selling Mo Johnston to Everton. Souness had always put him in ahead of Coisty, but the gaffer picked Ally who set off on an incredible run of scoring and struck up a partnership with Mark Hateley. At the time Coisty could have left – he only started as a sub even under Walter. But when he got in he took his chance and fought for his place. Under Souness he did well when he had an outing but was always the one left out. Walter was fair with him and by the end of the season he won both the big Player of the Year awards.

I've got to know Coisty well down the years. People see him

Foot on the ball out in the back garden at Wortley

A true Scot: in the kilt at sister Janette's wedding

Prize guy: picking up a ball from Leeds legend Eddie Gray
at the age of 12

ABOVE: Goal celebration with my pal Don Goodman (Reproduction by kind permission of *The Telegraph & Argus*, Bradford)

LEFT: McCall for England: holding the jersey with Bradford City chairman Stafford Heginbotham (Reproduction by kind permission of *The Telegraph & Argus*, Bradford)

So near and yet . . . Close to an England Under-21 debut,
but thankfully not close enough!
(© Bob Thomas Sports Photography)

Going up: Bradford's dressing-room celebrations after winning promotion
in 1985 (Reproduction by kind permission of
The Telegraph & Argus, Bradford)

Joy and tragedy: that fateful day we lifted the trophy before the disaster
(Reproduction by kind permission of *The Telegraph & Argus*, Bradford)

ABOVE: Scoring at Wembley: my last-gasp FA Cup final goal for Everton in 1989 (Reproduction by kind permission of *The Scottish Sun*, courtesy of Steve Welsh)

RIGHT: Get in there: a Rangers goal celebrated with the help of Mark Hateley (Reproduction by kind permission of *The Scottish Sun*, courtesy of Steve Welsh)

LEFT: Bloody hero! A cut head, but I can still smile (Reproduction by kind permission of *The Scottish Sun*, courtesy of Steve Welsh)

RIGHT: Voted player of the year at Rangers by McEwan's in my first season (Reproduction by kind permission of *The Scottish Sun*, courtesy of Steve Welsh)

as a happy-go-lucky character and this Golden Bollocks image. But as a person he has a deep desire to succeed. His decision to stay and do well under Walter showed that determination to be part of a new era. On the park he is not frightened of missing – you would see him blowing chances but he was always there for the next one. He was never afraid to make mistakes. Ally has a hunger to score goals and a self-confidence that when they come along he will find the net. When he was feeding off Hateley they were ideal together. We had also signed Dale Gordon from Norwich by then, someone who would be a big pal, and with the service from him, Miko and Peter Huistra there were goals galore that season.

I like to think I had a hand in Mo picking Everton as his next club. There were two or three others keen, like Leeds and Sheffield Wednesday. He asked what I thought of Howard Kendall and Howard Wilkinson, who was the Leeds boss. I knew about Mo's love of living life to the full, so I told him he would have a better relationship with Kendall. It would be a better blend than the strict discipline of Wilkinson. I told him that socially Kendall would be the one he could relax with and he could enjoy his life on and off the park. Under Wilko it would have been less fun.

Mo was different class. He was great for Scotland with Coisty, but what struck me about him was his fantastic fitness. I had heard the stories about him off the field, his liking for the fast life, but he is probably the hardest working striker I have ever played with. He was a goalscorer but also so unselfish for the side. Mo lived in Edinburgh and I only knew him for a few months, but he was a top lad. He was very much part of the dressing-room which was a happy place to be. He was one of the main characters and I never saw any resentment towards him because of the religious thing. It had died down by the time I arrived and I can say that he was a smashing player for Rangers.

The atmosphere at the club was great – no one was safe from being wound up. The Christmas party is a major event where everyone gets dressed up and tries their best to put on a show. Wee Ian Durrant told the new boys they had to get dressed up *before* they got to training, but we never fell for that one apart from the young keeper Colin Scott. He was spotted kitted out as Superman filling his car with petrol at a garage. The kids saw me leave with my clown's costume in my bag and I told them I would be back late and they would miss out on seeing me in the fancy dress. So they were a bit shocked to see the two Russians, Miko and Oleg Kuznetsov, back at the hotel in full fancy dress by the afternoon. Something had got lost in translation and the two had thought the meal was in the club canteen and went home early in disgust when the rest of us didn't arrive. Chenks was all done up like a Cossack, but none of the canteen ladies knew what to say to them to explain the 'do' was elsewhere. They had wasted £30 on fancy dress and their party was over by early afternoon. Try explaining that to Carly who saw them and couldn't figure why they could come back in fancy dress while daddy was out all night.

I was learning some of the 'language' too when I went out for a quiet drink one day with Chris Morris. He was a Cornish lad who played for Celtic and we got to know each other through our wives. He lived nearby and we used to have a game of snooker, but this time we stopped off in Shawlands for a quick one. As usual I made my excuses and went to the gents to let him buy the first round. The pub was nearly empty, but one of the customers followed me in and asked what I was doing out with that 'Fenian bastard'. I was taken aback, Chris was English. I went back to the bar and before I could tell Chris the tale he said that another guy had come up to him and asked what he was doing mixing with that 'orange bastard'. It just went to show that people could not understand that rival players can get on with each other, have a mutual respect and meet socially even when they play for opposite sides. It was a clear indication that you didn't go drinking with the enemy and from then on we were careful where we went.

For all the nastiness and aggression between the supporters the players usually get on well. We have a healthy respect for each other. When I played for Scotland I always looked on John Collins as a close friend. Over the years I have got to know Paul McStay and Tommy Boyd, plus Jackie McNamara and Tosh McKinlay lately. They have all been good colleagues. We are often asked to charity events, one from each side, and although there is rivalry and the banter gets going both sets of players know what it is like to be under the microscope and they have time for each other. Down the years I have bumped into Packie Bonner, Tommy Burns and Charlie Nicholas at various functions and we share stories. There is no bitterness at that level. One special memory was meeting the great Celtic legend Jimmy Johnstone and it was an honour to be in his company for half an hour. He was very lavish in his praise of Rangers and our achievements.

We had a couple of tasty matches with Celtic that March. We played them at home in the league when we had gone 20 games unbeaten with Coisty on a roll and we also drew them in the Scottish Cup semi. The first game was my first taste of defeat in the fixture and led to a night I won't forget. I had invited my brother Les and sister-in-law Jeanette to the game and we had booked a meal with my cousin Billy and his wife Marie in a Chinese restaurant that had been recommended to us. Everyone was down after the match, but the table was there for 8.30 p.m. so we still went out. To my amazement as we were strolling in this little Chinese guy came up to us and started shouting about how useless 'bloody Rangers' were. He took our coats into the cloakroom but came back with a Rangers scarf and proceeded to stamp on it in disgust, saying Rangers were 'bloody rubbish today'. It was the first time I had been to the restaurant and felt quite embarrassed for my family who thought it was extremely funny. The night went on and so did his verbal tirade and I finally snapped, promising him that in ten days time we would win and be celebrating. He was carried away too and said that we could bring all the players and their wives next time and get a free meal if we did win the semi. The strangest thing about the way he was ranting and raving was that it was meant, none of it was put on.

I got more of the same from a different angle the next morning on the way to training. I filled the car up with petrol and was queuing to pay when an attendant saw me and started smirking away. He sarcastically asked his pal what the Old Firm score was. I had to stand there and take the jibes. When I got to the till I paid and he said he was surprised I could afford it as I wouldn't be getting any bonuses for the game. It was relatively friendly stick but I knew then I didn't want to go through that too often.

We had to win that semi or else. It was live on Sky and pouring at Hampden. It was the night when Walter Smith's team came together. Yet it started so badly when Davie Robertson took his instructions too seriously. He was up against his old Aberdeen pal Joe Miller and Archie Knox told him to let him know he was in a game early on. Robbo certainly did and after about six minutes he took Joe down with a tackle round about his neck. He had to go. We were already without big Hateley, but Durranty dropped back deeper and Coisty played up front on his own. I would have taken a replay there and then, but just on half-time I won a clash with Brian O'Neill on halfway and went down the right before setting up Coisty. In a flash he scored. The Rangers End went delirious and so did we. Half-time was spent just getting our energy back. We knew there would be an onslaught and we weren't disappointed. They had the wind, the rain and an extra man behind them. It was a huge test of character for us and even then we would have settled for a draw. But we fought so hard and came together. Celtic hit the woodwork a couple of times, but we held on for a famous victory.

There were plenty of celebrations on the pitch and in the dressing-room. On the way back I remembered the Chinese man and called him to say he should book a table for 30. We never went, but he must have had an uncomfortable night. Luckily for him we had decided to stay in the town and went there instead. At least I had stuck to my word about the result. I also made sure I went back to that garage the next day for petrol, a vacuum and a car wash just to take the smile off the Celtic fan's face. I was angry he had taken the mickey so much, but it was sweet to get revenge. You have to lose an Old Firm game to realise how good it feels to win one.

We clinched the title against St Mirren with four games to go. It was just a question of when and not if but it was still nice to get my first medal. The boss left me out of the next game to make sure I didn't get booked or I would miss the Cup final with Airdrie. I had some trouble with refs at first and picked up four yellow cards in the opening eight games early on. I was on the brink of a ban even then but learned it was different to England. I was getting some silly bookings and it was a case of finding out what refs you could have a talk to and what ones just brandished a card. Jim McCluskey, one of our top officials, seemed to like booking me and gave me three yellows in as many games. Later on he became my favourite ref and the one most respected by the players.

The Rangers lads were characters and liked a bit of fun. The night before the last game at Aberdeen they had some. We needed one goal to make 100 for the season, but the title was won. A couple of the senior pros had a party, playing cards and having a couple of beers. I was tucked up in bed by 11 but my room-mate Dale Gordon heard a noise outside that soon died down. It wasn't until morning that the rumours went round about what went on. Archie Knox had got wind of the goings-on the night before and was prowling the corridors trying to find out where the party was. One of the boys said he had got a fright when he looked out of his room through the peephole and seen Archie's ear pressed hard against it to find out the culprits. Archie didn't have concrete proof but before the game, while the boss was out of the dressing-room, he made it pretty clear that he expected a good performance or there would be an inquest. With the final coming up one or two were worried as Archie was deadly serious about his threats. Thankfully we won 2–0 courtesy of the Golden Boy and finished with 101 goals . . . not to mention avoiding a Knox inquisition. It was only afterwards that Archie sneaked up to Coisty and captain Gough and said maybe that's the best way to prepare for games every Friday night! It was typical that Coisty should end up being the hero the next day.

The only let-down was the Cup final which was a poor spectacle. I felt guilty; we had put on such a poor show for the fans, but they had the double to celebrate for the first time in 11 years and I was soon told by everyone that the result mattered more than anything on these occasions. It was great to have two medals so quickly. I had gone to Everton in the hope of winning silverware, but there are no guarantees as I found out there. To cap it all I won the Rangers McEwan's Player of the Year award which I collected from Sandy Jardine.

The atmosphere in the dressing-room was outstanding, there were no cliques and bickering like Everton. Our form was consistent from people like Gary Stevens, Nigel Spackman and the unsung hero Scott Nisbet. There was even Euro 92 to look forward to with Scotland topping a tough group that included Rumania, Bulgaria and Switzerland. A draw between Rumania and Bulgaria put us through with the most precious point being a 2–2 we had pulled off from two down in Switzerland. There was character in that team too.

Chapter 11

One Tomas Brolin

W e flew out to America with Scotland just three days after the Cup final and it was a master stroke by Andy Roxburgh. The press critised the idea and the players were worried it would be too much travelling and hard work before the big event of the European Championship finals. Instead it was a real bonding exercise. One or two social activities brought the boys together and the first stop was Chicago where we found the John Hopkins Tower on our sight-seeing expedition. There were some sights seen by the end of that day. We took the lift to the top where there was a bar serving cocktails. Some bright spark had the idea that you drew tickets out of a hat to see what cocktail you would have next. You had to take what you had picked and there were some shockers. We got back to the hotel in happy mood. We felt more like a team already, and bumped into skipper Gough and Duncan Ferguson, an unlikely pairing, who had been sampling cocktails of their own. It was a good choice of venue because if we had gone anywhere else we would have been followed and not got away with it. Even the quiet lads like Paul McStay mixed and, of course, Coisty was his usual self

We went to Denver for a couple of days and played America in the famous Mile High Stadium. We won 1–0 on a humid day thanks to a Pat Nevin special. Next stop was Toronto which is a brilliant place to visit. The training was good and the togetherness was growing all the time. Some of the boys went on a helicopter trip to Niagara Falls, others to see the Bluejays baseball game. After we beat Canada 3–1 we all went out for a sing-song and it was one big happy family, Rangers and Celtic players included. We were on the back of a long, hard season but there was no tiredness because the training was good and we had time for rest and some recreation.

There was one game left, a 0–0 draw with Norway that was a bore. The team was taking shape and I was quietly confident of starting against Holland in the first game in the finals. It was a tough group, with Germany and also the CIS, but with the camaraderie I thought we could qualify for the second stage. Roxy stirred us up before the first game in Gothenburg by showing us a video of great achievements by Scots and told us we were making history as the first team to have played in these finals. The Dutch had top men in van Basten, Gullit and Dennis Bergkamp. I was to mark Frank Rijkaard, a tremendous player whom I managed to keep relatively quiet. It all went according to plan and we were looking good for a draw with Goughy even close to scoring. Then Gullit crossed, van Basten flicked on, Rijkaard knocked the ball down and Bergkamp scored. It took all of their top players working together to beat us. We had no chance to recover.

After the match Coisty and Stewart McKimmie were asked to do a dope test, but Stewart could not manage to fill his bottle so they had to get the next flight to Norrkopping which was our next base. Although we were down with the result we still had life in us as arch-prankster McCoist was to discover. His room was wrecked in his absence. There was toilet paper all over the room as if the Andrex puppy had been visiting. A player's most important item on these trips, the batteries for his TV remote control, were removed and hidden. Shaving foam was everywhere and sheets were tied up in knots. It is still a mystery to Coisty – he didn't know who stitched him up. It didn't matter, it was just sheer pleasure to see the top joker get well and truly turned over. Well done Juke Box (whoops!).

The humour was still alive and Brian Hendry, the SFA's

technical man, set up giant screens for us at our hideaway to watch other games, which helped kill any dead time. The serious side was to beat the Germans. If we had created two or three chances against the world champions we would have been delighted. But in the first half alone we had about a dozen attempts on their goal. We played with spirit, bravery and clever tactics. We carved them open, but they had their chances too in a game that was voted the best in the tournament.

Our chances all fell to defenders, much to the frustration of Coisty. He never really got a kick. We were unbelievably unlucky to be a goal down and then lost a second to a fluke from Effenberg just after the break. I even took a wee kick at him as he went past me celebrating. We should have at least scored in a game where we played superbly. It was a really cruel blow. We were out. The fans were great and stood by us at the end, even the neutrals were cheering us on. The reception they gave us made us proud and we wanted to give them a win before they went home. It would be a consolation for them and make their week. England lost to Sweden on the day Tomas Brolin became an honorary Scot and headed home before us for the first time ever.

The CIS had our two Rangers lads, Miko and Oleg, in the team and they revealed that their plan had been to draw their first two games and then beat us, the easy touches. They managed the first part and were taking it for granted they would beat Scotland. It was just a matter of turning up for them. They had already booked their accommodation for the next round.

At last we got the breaks we deserved and had been lacking in the opening games. Paul McStay's shot hit a post, then the keeper's head on its way in for our first goal of the finals. Brian McClair's effort was deflected too as we made it two and Gary McAllister's late penalty flattered us. If only we had been given that kind of luck just once in the earlier matches we would have qualified easily.

I saw the CIS team bus on the way out and couldn't help smiling. They had arrived full of themselves, with their wives and families all waiting for the comfortable win. Now their faces were stony. Our bus was a total contrast and I don't think Miko was too pleased when I picked him out for a wave and raised my glass to toast him. He had said beforehand that the champagne was cooling on their bus ready for the celebrations, but now he was choking. It wasn't champers for us, but it still tasted sweet.

We all went out for a farewell party afterwards and the whole squad was in top form. We were treated like royalty at a local club. The Scots and the Swedes had got on famously and had struck up a great rapport. It didn't take Coisty long to get on stage and launch into his Bruce Springsteen impressions, while big Derek Whyte did Leroy Brown. The rest of us settled for a chorus of 'There's only one Tomas Brolin'. Even Archie Knox turned up for a beer or three. We could enjoy it because we finally got what we deserved. We said our goodbyes the next day knowing we had done Scotland proud. I couldn't wait for the next one and felt sure we would do well in the World Cup. The midfield trio of myself, Paul McStay and Gary McAllister all came away with praise ringing in our ears, but for me Richard Gough was the star of the show. It was a great squad effort and Andy Roxburgh and Craig Brown deserve every credit for engineering such an atmosphere in the camp.

Chapter 12

Simply the best

I couldn't have been happier with my life at the start of the '92–'93 season. I had made the right move and was on a high on the back of the finals. There were even stories in the papers that the Italians liked me and I was talked about as a possible £3.5 million target for one of the Serie A sides. It was never on my mind.

We played nine games in August, which could only happen in Scotland. A shock 4–3 defeat by Dundee sparked one of the best runs at home and in Europe in the club's history. Walter kept most of the team together but added Davie McPherson who had starred for Scotland in the summer. We put Lyngby out of Europe and were drawn with Stuttgart in the final qualifier before the new Champions League. But because they had played an ineligible player against Leeds they had to replay and lost, so the great Battle of Britain was on. We had gone 12 games without defeat, so taking on Leeds held no fears for us. I had even got a couple of goals myself against Partick Thistle and Hearts.

The hype before the Leeds game was incredible. I was right in the middle of it, the boy from Leeds who played for Rangers. It was also strange because there were to be no away fans at either leg for security reasons. However, there were certain deals done and a few managed to beat the ban. Still the noise at Ibrox for the first game was the loudest I have ever heard. I had butterflies, though it was more anticipation than nerves. But the whole place went quiet – you could hear the proverbial pin drop – when my mate Gary smacked one in so early. Walter had told me before the game to play left side and stop Gordon Strachan. I wasn't too pleased about that as I wanted to press forward, but it was a kind of backhanded compliment. After Gary's goal that plan went out of the window. I wanted to have a crack at David Batty, Gary Speed and Macca. Durranty moved to the left and got forward and we got right back into the game. It was close and then John Lukic punched a corner into his own goal. We were rampant and Super Ally scored a second. I put Mark Hateley in late on but he had run out of legs and couldn't take the chance. At the end the applause was only muted – the fans thought it wasn't enough. But the lads did. We thought we could go down there and get goals.

Straight afterwards we started reading reports from the English press and John Sadler in the *Sun* in particular writing us off. They ran down the Scottish game and said we would get sorted out in Leeds. I was also disappointed that the Scots who used to play for Leeds, Billy Bremner, Peter Lorimer and Eddie Gray, were lining up to say how many we would lose by at Elland Road.

We would use those words to our advantage later, but we had no time to dwell on that result as we were playing Aberdeen in the Skol Cup final a few days later. They were our big rivals that season and beating them would also lift us in the league. Theo Snelders, their keeper, got caught out by the new backpass law and one hit him on the chest when he wasn't able to catch it. The ball broke away from him and I was following through to score the first goal through his legs. This is a feat I have often reminded him of since he moved to Rangers. To be fair, Aberdeen came back well and equalised. Going into extra-time they were favourites. Goughy was off injured and I was back at right-back. The Leeds game had taken its toll, but we hung on in and Gary Smith's own goal won us the Cup. As well as scoring I got the man of the match prize, which was not bad for a right-back.

We were well fired up for the Leeds return. It was the most important game of my career. We trained at the ground and dad turned up to watch. He wasn't going to the game but wished me all the best and told me to enjoy it. I was playing for him and my family. There was pressure on me, but they felt it more than anyone. Les and Alan and my sister Janette had been taking stick at work, my nieces and nephews – Jane, Karen, John, Chris and Alex – were being slaughtered at school. Dad was coming in for some flak at his local club. At least I was able to do something about it. They could only wait and hope. I got tickets for Les and Alan thanks to a swap arrangement with Gary McAllister. We got round the blanket ban and were not the only ones. I saw a lad called Chic, a big Rangers fan, walking to the ground with a Leeds scarf on and laughed. Rangers fans in disguise!

We did to Leeds what they had done to us and hit them with a quick goal. Mark Hateley hit a superb drive past Lukic. The keeper took a lot of blame – the ball went in at the middle of the goal – but he was caught out by the speed of the shot and the surprise factor. Leeds made chances – Eric Cantona missed a couple and Andy Goram was outstanding. John Brown was immense as we stood firm and soaked up the pressure. With half an hour to go we got a classic counter attack goal with big Mark crossing on the run and Coisty heading a great second. Leeds needed four goals to beat us and although they got one from Cantona, Goram was not letting any more by him.

In the final seconds I was battling for a corner down at the Leeds Kop end where I had stood for years. The crowd were screaming Yorkshire reject at me and I turned round and showed them the score with my hands. Honest. I think they took the gesture the wrong way. At the final whistle their fans stood and applauded us which was gracious. It was an acknowledgement of a performance that was one of our best.

There was so much at stake that night. If you look at what happened to Leeds that season you know what it meant. They went to pieces, finished 17th in the league and could not get over it. It was such a game that the after-effects were huge.

I'm just glad it wasn't us who lost as I dread to think what would have happened to us. It was one of the best nights of my career and my favourite moment because of the place where we did the business.

We were also on the biggest bonuses the club had offered, £12,000 a man, to win, but that didn't matter as much as the result. It could not compare to that glowing feeling. The hype and the fact we had beaten England's best was a wonderful feeling. There is nothing better than being put down and bouncing back like that. The result meant so much to people in Scotland, but I know it was also well received by my folk round Leeds. All of them were at work or school that few minutes earlier the next day, putting the result up on the noticeboard or in the playground and having the final say. I savoured the journey on the way to Manchester where we talked a nightclub into staying open for us and our friends and families before we flew home the next day. I just let it all sink in. My pal Mark Ellis from Bradford came over to join in the celebrations and it was a result cheered back there too. I had so much mail from old fans wanting us to beat Leeds. It was a big thing in Manchester as the locals don't like Leeds either, so they joined in the merriment. Durranty's pals were there and Coisty's, John Brown had some mates out and it went on until six in the morning. Every Rangers song written was sung. On the way out a big bouncer told me he had seen some after-hours parties but never anything like ours.

When we made it to the hotel it was still full of Rangers punters. As I got back to my room I was shocked to find Dale had let a couple of Bomber Brown's pals kip in my bed. There were bodies everywhere, most clutching bottles of champagne in their sleep. It was a bomb site. We were due up in a couple of hours so I just took a bottle of champagne and headed for the foyer to take it all in. Davie Dodds, one of the coaches, was there too. About eight in the morning the gaffer came out of a lift, walked up to us and had a real go at Doddsy for letting me stay up all night. I told him not to worry, it was only Celtic on Saturday. He turned, grinned and said: 'Make sure you finish the champers then.' There was no coming down off Cloud Nine. I still sweat thinking about that night.

We won 1–0 at Parkhead – Durranty scored the winner and the ball kept rolling. Next up was Marseille at Ibrox in the Champions League opener. For the first 75 minutes we never played at all. Coisty was missing. We had kids like Neil Murray and Stephen Pressley playing, with young Gary McSwegan trying his best up front. The three-foreigner rule they had in Europe at the time did not help us much either. Somehow Hateley and McSwegan scored with late headers and we scrambled a draw. Character again. We knew we had to do better to do anything in Europe and the next game was against CSKA Moscow in Bochum. We had 6,000 fans in a 9,000 crowd. Ian Ferguson's goal gave us a precious win.

The league was going smoothly with a win over Celtic and I got a goal against Dundee United. The secret was just spirit and confidence. It was all for one and one for all again. We didn't have an outstanding individual in the side. We had five or six people having their best seasons at the same time in an all-round superb side. That was the best Rangers team I played in. The number of times we went behind and still got something out of games said it all about what we had among us. We would pull things round – it was just a matter of time. We had been outplayed by a team like Marseille and clawed our way back. We were flying going into the Bruges games and thought a win and a draw would set us up for the Marseille return. We went to Belgium without Fergie, Stevens and Gordon. They had not lost at home for three years and we still got a point with Peter Huistra equalising when I miskicked one across the goal. The Belgian skipper Frankie van der Elst said we were close to being good enough to win the European Cup and he singled me out as the outstanding player in the group.

He thought they should build a team around me. I was a bit surprised that someone should be so complimentary and as you can imagine I took some awful abuse back home for that one. It was one of our best second-half performances – they hardly got out of their half. We were kicking ourselves not to have won. It was one of my best games for the club and I had another one to come in the home leg.

Our chances in the Ibrox game were hit when Mark Hateley was sent off for smacking one of their boys. It was just before half-time and we were down to ten men and up against it. We had the lead thanks to Durranty who was brilliant that season. If ever you wanted someone for a big game it was him. He was always good for a goal in those type of matches too. It was great to have him back at his best after that knee injury that robbed him of top football for so long. We were tiring in the second half and Bruges equalised, but that was the cue for big Nissy to make his name. He played a one-two with my backside and was trying to cross the ball I think. It flew in the air, bounced and fooled their keeper before going in. The ball was sucked in by the fans and we held on for a precious win.

The next weekend was a sad one for big Scott Nisbet and the club. We went to Parkhead well ahead in the league, but obviously not wanting to lose. We went down 2–1 and Nissy played his last game for the club before quitting with a pelvic injury. I had roomed with him early on and he was a big, honest lad. He was Rangers through and through. He loved the club and would have given everything for them. He had struggled for a while and played through the pain. He was just getting through games, but no one thought it would finish him.

Although we lost and the unbeaten run was over we got a massive ovation from our fans at the end. It was their way of saying thanks for what we had put together that season. They were paying their respects even after a defeat by the old enemy. We beat Aberdeen in the league and Hearts in the Cup semi, Just days before the Marseille match. The resilience of the squad was being tested but we stood up to it and each game was bigger than the last.

Before we left for Marseille I was voted Scottish Player of the Month and the boss got the manager's award. But we were without suspended Hateley and Durranty played up with Coisty. It was, in effect, the semi-final of the European Cup. A win would put us through, a defeat would put us out. A draw would take it to the last group match with us still having a chance. For the umpteenth time we went behind with Suazee scoring a beauty. But there was no panic, we had been behind before and come good. Durranty belted in an equaliser and it was a fair result. We matched them home and away, a side that had class like Rudi Voller, Didier Deschamps and Marcel Desailly. They were strong and yet we had gone there and battled with them. We could still make the final if they drew or lost in Bruges and we beat CSKA at Ibrox. We were that close.

The CSKA game was strange. Coisty had three acceptable chances early on and headed them all over. We heard Marseille were winning and the place went quiet. There were no more cheers, so we guessed they had won. In a way it was a relief as I would hate to think we had missed out by not beating Moscow. We were at the end of our batteries. That night they ran out – we had given everything. The ovation at the end was touching. There were tears all round and we had a lap of honour that made you think we had won the European Cup itself. There was pride among the crying. Coisty and Goughy were caught up in the emotion of it. Our attitude was that we could do better next time, be stronger, more experienced and ready to cope. We didn't know that was as near as we would get in our careers. It was never to be again – that was a one-off. Because of the stress we had put ourselves through it would also take its toll on our bodies and maybe minds the season after. The likes of myself, Bomber, Slim and Andy Goram all played with injuries that would eventually need operations. They were little niggles and didn't seem to matter at the time, but by carrying on we were making it worse. No one wanted to back out of those games, we went match to match just marching on. Rest would have cured many of those problems, but you didn't want to miss a game as they were all huge. You don't think of it at the time, you just keep on going, but it catches you in the end. In my case a little tear got worse and I needed a hernia operation at the start of the new season. Those ops cost us the chance of glory that next time.

Still we had gone ten games undefeated in Europe and were in with a chance of a domestic treble. We won the title at Airdrie with a Gary McSwegan goal. The next few games drifted by as a few of us were rested. In the final game at Falkirk I was made captain for the first time, a big honour to end a memorable campaign. We headed off for Monaco for a break.

The Scottish Cup final was against our old rivals Aberdeen who must have been sick of the sight of us. We beat them 2–1 although it was not one of our better displays. Winning the treble at Parkhead was special for the fans and the most successful season the club has probably had came to a close.

I don't think there has ever been a side with better spirit. Our record shows 44 games unbeaten in domestic football and ten in Europe. I was even nominated in the last four of the PFA Player of the Year awards with Andy Goram, Coisty and John Collins. In my eyes it had to be the keeper's prize and it was. I also won the *Scottish Football Today* magazine's trophy, voted by the fans, and the *Rangers News* Player of the Year. That was undoubtedly my best season and it was pleasing to know other people thought the same.

Chapter 13

Red Adair

If the season with Rangers was memorable, then it was forgettable when it came to Scotland. I was so looking forward to getting back with the lads after the Euro finals and getting on the World Cup trail. The group was tough – Italy, Portugal and our old foes Switzerland, with the first game in Berne. Normally you would be happy with a draw there but on the back of the Swedish finals we fancied ourselves for a win and that was our downfall. They took the lead, Coisty equalised and we thought we could go on for victory. Andy Roxburgh wanted a calmer approach, but the belief among us was so good that we went for a win and got caught. It was our confidence that led to us being carried away. Our best team lost 3–1 and we had Richard Gough sent off for handball. People laughed at the time when he said the ball hit a sprinkler, but I saw it happen and it's true. The boss gave us a dressing-room blast for going against orders and quite rightly so.

We trooped back to the hotel after the game and that's when the trouble began. Usually we fly home straightaway but we couldn't get a flight. Most of us decided to go into the village we were staying in for a couple of quiet beers. Jock Brown, the TV commentator and brother of Craig, spotted us and reported back. Craig was sent to tell us to go back to the hotel because it wouldn't look good to be out drinking after such a result.

Big Duncan Ferguson was among us. He had been with the under-21s, and I don't think he wanted to go to bed early. He nicked a pushbike and had a laugh riding on it on the way back to the hotel. Roxy called a meeting when we got back and told us if we wanted to drown our sorrows to go to a room downstairs where there was a fridge with some beers in it. He didn't want us drinking in public, which was fair enough. Unfortunately for some of the boys the fridge was too well stocked and they took what was available. If we had stayed in that local pub we would have been off in a hour, but some of the lads decided to go for it with all this free beer. Durranty was with the squad and had come on as sub. He was cracking his usual one-liners and Coisty was up to mischief. Big Fergie was the butt of their humour and messing around. He was the new boy after all.

I was rooming with Gary McAllister and I finally made it to my bed, only to be woken up soon after by the bold Gary rolling in the worse for wear and making a loud entry. Then there was another banging and I looked out to see the dream ticket of Durie and Ferguson making for their room next to ours. Coisty and Durranty were also coming in with the wee man giving big Duncan a final insult or two before heading for bed. I was awake again by now and decided to block McCoist and Durrant in their room. I knew they would be late for checking out, so I thought I would make life harder for Coisty in particular. He would have jumped up late, wanting to make a panicking bid for the bus, opened the door and been greeted by all this Swiss woodwork stopping him. Juke Box was the main furniture remover, finding loads of chairs and bookcases in this old corridor to stack up outside the McCoist and Durrant lodgings. I thought this was a great idea, Coisty would get out eventually and as a prankster he would see the funny side. I went to bed with a chuckle.

But I didn't realise Fergie had been the victim of one trick too many. He had gone to bed, only to find it was covered in peanuts, left by either Coisty or the boy Durrant. The big man had enough and was in the hallway, still full of bravado. He was pretending to strike a lighter against the chairs. 'I'll teach these b*******,' he muttered. I don't think he meant it – I don't believe for one minute he wanted to set fire to the wood, but there were scorch marks on one of the chairs before we told him it wasn't such a bright idea. I took the lighter off him to earn the new nickname Red Adair.

I thought that was the end of the story but the next morning I heard hoovering outside and there was Craig Brown trying to sort out the mess. He was trying to clean up the peanuts and told the lads to get the furniture back. Coisty and Durranty opened the door and just collapsed in heaps at the furniture stacked outside. Andy Roxburgh didn't share the joke. He called another meeting and told us he was disappointed at the behaviour of one or two of the players. Word got back to Ibrox and there was a picture there to greet me with my head and Coisty's cut out and put on a poster of *Backdraft*, the movie about firemen that was popular at the time. Later on Coisty and Durranty were wound up that I had saved their lives, but it wasn't really that bad. There was no real harm done, apart from a couple of burns on some old chairs. The story just grew and grew, but I can put that record straight.

The group went from bad to worse. We drew at home with Portugal and Italy at Ibrox, games I missed through injury. We didn't have a national home with Hampden being rebuilt and it didn't feel right. The Hampden roar was replaced by the Ibrox squeak. The atmosphere was nowhere near as partisan as we were used to at Hampden. It was at a stage when club supporters didn't get behind the national side, so the whole thing was a flop.

We went to Portugal in April and that really was a low point. We needed to win to have any chance of going through. The preparations started badly when Craig Brown apparently heard Rui Barros wasn't playing because some taxi driver had told him. Well, he did and he ripped us to pieces. We went one down early on but Kevin Gallacher had a good goal disallowed for an offside that wasn't. Instead they scored again on half-time, which was a major boot in the privates.

It was a long walk along the tunnel to the dressing-room at Lisbon's Stadium of Light. We sat there in silence as the boss said his piece. We just wanted to save face in the second half, but it got off to a bizarre start. As we were walking out I saw Craig Brown stooping down, scrambling after Jim McInally to try and put black boot polish on his tie-ups. Craig is a real stickler for details and thought the white tie-ups against our socks looked wrong. That's the way Craig is, he likes you to have your shirt inside your shorts and be smart and represent your country properly. Paul McStay had also suffered because of that as he sometimes had to wear cycle pants to protect an injury, something Craig didn't like as they clashed with his shorts, so the cycle pants came off for games. These tie-ups were obviously annoying him too and he thought it was unprofessional, like a pub team. I don't know how many noticed the incident, but it was quite unnerving to see Craig on his hands and knees. He was trying to uphold Scotland's image, but it was the last thing on Jim's mind.

We collapsed in the second half and Portugal were four up in no time. Poor old Coisty broke his leg before they made it five. I had been in games with him before when he had gone off squealing like a pig and was back on in minutes, but this time was different. I thought he had just had a wee fright, but he really did get hurt.

My own personal philosophy was to go down fighting. I wanted some pride back, so I ran all the way to the end. Paolo Sousa wanted to swap shirts at the finish but I refused. I had seen enough of his jersey and didn't want a reminder of a horror night. But he came back and was respectful rather than patronising, so I gave him my top in the tunnel. The dressing-room was like a morgue. Losing was bad enough but Coisty's leg break made it worse. The defeat was a nightmare and for the next few days we were slaughtered. The press singled me out as a rare success and I was embarrassed as they said Craig Levein and I were the only ones to escape criticism.

It was only later that I found out those sentiments were not shared by the management team. A top official on the backroom staff told me they thought I had gone about like a headless chicken late in the game. In fact Roxy and Craig thought I was one of the reasons we took a hammering. They thought I had lost my discipline and was at fault for the heavy defeat. It was said in the aftermath of the match and I was hurt and disappointed at those comments. There had been times in my career where I probably deserved that headless chicken remark, but not this one. I wouldn't accept that opinion as it was only at 4–0 that I started tearing about looking for a consolation. That was seen by many as being proof of my commitment and refusal to give in. I was stunned to hear that I had been knocked behind my back. Over the years I learned that the best way to say things was to your face and not to others. More so because if things are explained to you then you have the chance to put them right, you can take it in and do something about it. You need to be told sometimes or you will never improve. I would have been happier to have heard those comments from them directly.

It soured my thoughts about Andy Roxburgh. I never had a run-in with him – he picked me and gave me my chance – but this left a bad taste. Ironically I never played for him again after that because I had injuries and then he left when we failed to go through. His organisation and preparation were meticulous. He was very proud to be Scotland's manager and conveyed that to the players. From my point of view I enjoyed my time under him. The two finals I played under him were good fun and great times. People thought we would never have that rapport as Andy was seen as a school teacher, but he gave us freedom and was reasonably successful as a Scotland manager.

Chapter 14

A hard act to follow

Rangers were coming off the back of a wonder season on the park, but domestically things were not so successful for me. My wife Liz had become an aerobics teacher which was very time-consuming, but something she felt she wanted to do rather than sit about the house being a footballer's wife, which I could fully understand. With Rangers going so well I was being invited to functions, dinners and all the usual events for Player of the Year ceremonies. We were drifting apart and that's what happened. In the summer we took a long holiday in America and Mexico. We agreed that a parting of the ways, a separation, was best for everyone. There was an unhealthy atmosphere at home at times and it was for the best. It was the hardest decision I have ever had to make, but it was the right one and needed to be done. It has worked out as the correct one. It was February before we finally sold the house in Newton Mearns but we both still moved to within a mile of it. We both went on to remarry, Liz to a good lad called Scott, while I was lucky enough to meet Tracey. The kids are doing great and that was massively important to me. They live close by. I see as much of them after the split as I want to and we are in touch every day. My folks had split up when I was young and so had Liz's, when she was 11. We had been together for over ten years and were just looking for something different, but in the end it was amicable. Coming to Glasgow probably was the beginning of the end – having such a successful season was maybe the final straw. Liz and Scott have had two children of their own, while Tracey has presented me with my little boy Craig and daughter Victoria.

I moved into a club flat near Haggs Castle for a while. It was the only real disruption I suffered. Carly and Lee just treat it now as though they have two houses, two mums and two dads. The big relief is that they are fine. Carly is a gem, a girl of ten going on 20 and a mother hen to all the others. Lee is a typical boy who enjoys his football. When he first went to Ibrox it was only for Broxy Bear, but now he is into the game itself. After some games some of the players' kids go on the pitch while we unwind in the lounge. Gordon Durie's boy Scott was going down the wing and crossing for Mark Hateley's lad Tom to nod them in or trying to beat Lewis Goram. Brian Laudrup's kid Nikolai was keeping the ball up in the centre circle and there was Lee sliding all over the park like his dad. He always comes in with his trousers dirty – you know he's my boy because he has green stains along the back of his pants. Before I can tell him off he reminds me he was playing like his old fella. It's funny how boys copy their dads. Durranty's lad Max and Coisty's youngster Alex are also to be found talking a good game. It is obviously in the blood.

We started that season in our Italian base of Il Ciocco when the news came in about Duncan Ferguson joining us. Big Mark Hateley refused to believe it. He thought we didn't need him. A few days later Fergie signed and Mark still couldn't figure out why Rangers would spend £4 million on a striker and not play him. It was unlikely those two would be a combination and Mark was stunned by the news. It must have got him going because the big man went on to have his finest season for the club. He carried us in a lot of games and won matches on his own.

There were stories of a rift between Fergie and Mark, but all the stuff about him cutting up his Versace shirts were news to me. They had the odd arm-wrestle but that was it. There was never any violence that I saw. Mark was definitely threatened in another way by Duncan. When he got back to Ibrox he changed his training number from 14 to ten. Fergie had been down for the number ten but was swapped instead to 14. You could tell there was an edge between them. Mark was just determined to keep that shirt. Mark felt he still had some good years left in him and picked up the gauntlet.

The man Mark went to for his change of numbers was Jimmy Bell, our bus driver, kit man and unofficial president of the Ian Durrant fan club. He had an Aladdin's cave deep inside the ground where he kept all the boots, trainers and leisure wear. Trying to get a new pair of laces off him was like getting blood out of a stone. Durranty would always get anything he wanted, but I had to go down to Jimmy's 'office'. It was also a shrine to the great Rangers players in his thoughts. I went in pre-season and saw all these pictures of his favourites. There was Davie Cooper, Terry Butcher, Ray Wilkins, Graeme Souness, Chris Woods, Coisty and of course Durranty. I said to him that I saw I wasn't up there. I used to kid him it took a wee ginger-haired lad from Yorkshire to win a double and then a treble and yet he had all these pictures of Butcher, Souness and company who didn't do that for him. Jimmy turned round and said: 'That was good, but what do you do for an encore?' It hit home – what could we do next? The only thing left was a back-to-back treble and reaching the final in Europe. It sunk in that this was going to be a difficult season. The consolation was that the next time I went down to Jimmy's room there was a picture of me slapped up in the middle. I had arrived after all. Cheers, Jim.

It was a tough start. Andy Goram was out with knee problems and would miss two-thirds of the season. Coisty was sidelined with his leg break, Bomber Brown and I had injuries. A big part of that successful side was missing. I had my hernia op on 13 August and within a month I was back playing against Levski Sofia in the European Cup. The boss asked me if I was ready after a couple of days' training and, because of the injuries and the importance of the tie, I said I would give it a go. I was skipper for the night but we threw the game away. We were 2–0 up and then 3–1 before it finished 3–2. They were sloppy goals to lose and proved costly. We were still holding on comfortably in the return and it was freak 30-yarder in injury time that put us out. After the highs of the previous season this was a massive low.

The only real highlights of that season were the Celtic games. We even met them in the Coca-Cola Cup semis when the boss pulled a fast one. We had to toss to decide the venue. Joe Jordan got the first one right and the gaffer said that was just to decide who would call for the real one. 'It's your shout then,' he said and this time Jordan called and got it wrong. So instead of Parkhead it was Ibrox after the boss had thought on his feet. That was also the cause of my first real taste of fan bitterness. I was out for a quiet beer when I was approached by a Celtic fan calling me a 'lucky orange bastard'. As I was injured and recovering from my operation I didn't feel too lucky at the time. He was talking about the boss's double-cross with the coin. I then told him we would be as well playing at Parkhead with our record and just as he was calming down at my words of reason I pitched in with 'and we'll play you with ten men again if you want', referring back to our last Cup meeting.

On the night, Peter Huistra got sent off and my mind flashed back to my words of a few days before. Me and my big mouth were saved by Mark Hateley who got the winner for us with a man short. We won the final against Hibs at Parkhead with Supersub McCoist scoring a spectacular winner but leaving a large dent in the penalty box where he landed.

We were definitely feeling the backlash of the European exit and lost to Celtic in the league before going there at New Year and winning a cracker 4–2. They were favourites for that one, but we won comfortably with early goals from big Mark and two from Miko helping us along. It was a funny season – we were always better than anyone else without being special. We were chasing the treble again but it was a flat time. Even making the Scottish Cup final after beating Kilmarnock in a replay did not feel too exciting.

The way we won the title summed it up, not winning one of

the final five games and even clinching the championship with a 1–0 defeat at Hibs. We were still expected to beat Dundee United in the final, but never played anything like we could and lost to a comical goat when Ally Maxwell and Davie McPherson got in a tangle. It sounds crazy but it was a disappointing season even with two of the three major trophies to our name. Going out of Europe haunted us all the way through. The fatigue from the previous season was also holding us back. Mark Hateley was the exception to the general rule and was the only choice for all the Player of the Year awards.

The signing of Fergie did not pay off. He used to come in, do his training and then go off. I felt sorry for him. Rangers bought him early because they were under pressure with other teams trying to buy him from Dundee United. Ideally they would have left him there for another year, but he came and with his injuries and big Mark's form he never really got a chance. The head-butting incident with John McStay did him no favours, but that was down to frustration. If he had come later in his career I believe he would have been a legend.

On the Scotland front Craig Brown had taken over as boss. The first game under him was in Italy and I went there on the brink of signing a new deal for Rangers. The last words Walter Smith told me were, 'Don't come back here injured or else.' He wasn't anti the Scotland team, he just had a lot of players returning from international duty with knocks and was sick of it. I went with a dead leg and could have pulled out, but I wanted to play and I was fit enough to start. But Dino Baggio landed on my ankle in the last minute and I was in pain and had to miss the next Rangers game. The gaffer blanked me for weeks after that. Although my injury was minor it was another problem for him and the contract talks went on ice. Nothing was mentioned about a new deal for months. I think it was the boss's way of letting me know who paid my wages. He never stopped me going on Scotland duty, but the message came through clearly. The contract came through eventually in December. I missed several Scotland games later, but they were down to genuine injuries.

We finished the season with a World Cup warm-up game in Holland. We owed them a game because they had opened the new Hampden, but it was a nightmare. They were coming out of a training camp while most of our lads had been on a two-week break at least at the end of their seasons. We were battered 3–1 although it was memorable as this was the last time Ruud Gullit played for his country. He went off at half-time after being in my pocket for 45 minutes (I wish!) but Holland still ran rings round us and gave us a doing.

I couldn't wait for the season to end. At least it went out with a bang. Ian Durrant was having his stag night and Coisty was going to Canada for a testimonial dinner, so they pulled together and we all headed out for a long party. Juke Box, Ian Ferguson and I flew in from Holland to Glasgow to take off and join in the fun. There were guys from Coisty's committee and the TV presenter Dougie Donnelly plus TV star and impressionist Jonathon Watson. There were only so many tickets available to fly straight to Toronto and I won the toss to go direct (and club class too). The next nine hours were hilarious. I was with wee Johnny Watson who is a great mimic. He asked me who I liked him doing best and I said Denis Law was my favourite. He was in full flow after a couple of drinks and helped me get over my treble depression. But after four hours of Denis Law I told the wee man to go back to being himself. The trouble was he wasn't sure who he was any more and was talking some strange new language and still sounding like Denis Law. We touched down and because of the time difference it was just lunchtime. The boys who were already there were just about to start Durranty's stag do. After a quick shower we were ready to go again and even wee Johnny was sobering up. We had a pool competition for a couple of hours and, unknown to Jonathon, Andy Goram was covering his face in blue chalk every time he went up to him to slap his cheeks. As the night went on he looked just like a wee drunk Smurf. After going to the bar he was quite proud to tell everyone that he must be famous in Canada because everyone was pointing at him and laughing. He thought he had been recognised. He even thought it was funny that he had seen John Brown at the bar and he had blue chalk on his nose, but was telling people to keep it quiet. He thought that was a good joke.

The whole trip was great tonic after a long season, we were well looked after and went everywhere in limos – baseball, games of golf and the odd fishing trip. Coisty was in his element at his testimonial dinner and with his pal, ex-*Superstars* TV show winner Brian Budd, he set up Durranty at the bar. They were ordering three Tequila slammers at a time and knocking them back. They had got through about five when Durranty smelled a rat. He was absolutely sozzled, while Coisty and his mate were stone cold sober despite their exotic drinks. It was only when he offered Durranty his 'Tequila' at the sixth round that he realised it was only tap water. Durranty had been well done by those two and the barman.

The boys had a great week with Simple Minds member Derek Forbes and wee Cliff, Coisty's pal, keeping us in stitches with their patter and singalongs. The only low point of the tour was when Coisty's mate Andy Knox had his pockets picked while looking round Toronto. Anyone who knows Knoxy will be aware that this is nearly impossible as he has padlocks on his pockets and a secret code on his wallet. Whoever did it must have been very professional.

The nearest I got to the World Cup in 1994 was being in America with Tracey to meet some of her relatives. They also had ten relatives over from Glasgow to support the Republic of Ireland. We got talking about football and I asked them if the Republic played Scotland which country would they support. Eight of them said the Irish, one said a draw and the other said Scotland. I thought that was strange as they were all born in Scotland. I was just about to get on my high-horse and tell them what I thought when one of the lads asked who I would want to win if England met Scotland – after all I was born in England. I got the point and saw that issue in a new perspective.

I had a good close season and felt refreshed for the new one. Not only had I been to Canada, I had a holiday in America and went with Tracey and the kids to Eurodisney, so I was raring to go. Rangers had signed Basile Boli and Brian Laudrup. Boli came with a good reputation and had helped Marseille win the European Cup, while Brian's brother Michael was more famous but he was still rated a top talent. Unfortunately our first competitive game that season was in Europe, away to AEK Athens in Greece. The boss sprang a surprise by dropping John Brown and Dave McPherson, playing Stephen Pressley with Gary Stevens pushed into the middle beside him. We were lucky still to be in the tie, losing 2–0, because we were humped.

The bonuses were now £20,000 a man because the money at stake in the Champions League was increasing all the time, but it was no spark for us as we went into one of the most depressing weeks in recent history. We lost at home to AEK, then were slammed 2–0 by Celtic before going out at home to Falkirk in the Coca-Cola Cup. The alarm bells were ringing loudly and there were rumblings about the new boys, Boli and Laudrup, who had only joined for their European experience. Both of them had struggled to settle early and Brian gave no evidence that he was to become a legend. At the start he had a shocker – you gave him the ball all the time and he did nothing with it. Basile was more outgoing, but there were constant rumours that he did not fancy the training or the tactics and it was making the newspapers back in France that he was unhappy. That talk alienated him from the rest of the lads. It was the first time we had big-name foreigners come in and although there was not any us and them situation going on everyone was being judged on their merits and they did not have much to shout about.

Going out of Europe had people talking about the financial implications for the club, but for the players it was a big blow. We had so many great memories of the successful season in Europe and it was tough going through this season without those dates to spice it all up. When you win the league by so many points it can get a bit run-of-the-mill. We were winning titles with four or five games to go and I was honestly looking around hoping for a better challenge so it would be more exciting. The only place we found that extra buzz was Europe and that had gone for another year. That was why our performances suffered. The season before I arrived Rangers had only clinched the title on the last day against Aberdeen and I was longing for that kind of close finish.

This time we won the championship by 15 points from Motherwell and Hearts. Dundee United and Aberdeen were in trouble. They had been serious competition in the past, but United went down and Aberdeen stayed up through the play-offs. The only thing that got us going were critics asking if our dominance was going after that bad start. That brought the ranks together and we battled through it. A win at Parkhead in October by 3–1 told us we were back on the rails again. That was also the debut of Alan McLaren who came from Hearts in a swap for Slim McPherson. I had always rated McLaren and he had an outstanding first match that suggested my faith in him was right.

I first saw Alan on Scotland under-21 duty and I picked him out straightaway as a high-class defender. He was also a stand-out for Hearts, playing with older guys like Craig Levein and McPherson. He was solid and although I rated the other two highly even then he looked better. I knew he was a Scotland player from the first time I saw him.

We beat Motherwell on New Year's Eve in a crucial game and I remember Lee asked me on the morning of the match if there was any chance of me scoring a goal as he hadn't seen too many from me. He was getting some stick at school about his dad not getting any goals like Hateley and Laudrup. Strangely enough I got the first one in a 3–1 win and had such faith that I even put money on myself that day at 16 to 1.

The boss had signed Alex Cleland and Gary Bollan from Dundee United and had one of his 'team spirit trip' ideas to help the new boys settle. They headed off to Monaco and the gaffer took great delight in telling the lads who needed treatment that they couldn't go. He informed the likes of myself, Goram, Brown and McCoist that we were not allowed to go. He had a big smile as he thought that would make sure there was no nonsense going on over there.

Goal-crazy: a McCall special goes in against Dundee United
(Reproduction by kind permission of *The Scottish Sun*,
courtesy of Steve Welsh)

ABOVE: What have I told you about diving in, Ruud? Mr Gullit loses out on a fifty-fifty ball (Reproduction by kind permission of *The Scottish Sun*, courtesy of Steve Welsh)

RIGHT: What's it like to score a goal? Mo Johnston and I enjoy the World Cup win over Sweden (Reproduction by kind permission of *The Scottish Sun*, courtesy of Steve Welsh)

Only happy when we're holding trophies:
Durranty and I lap it up (Reproduction by kind permission of *The Scottish Sun*, courtesy of Steve Welsh)

Let the party begin! The three must-get-beers enjoy
beating Leeds in Europe (Reproduction by kind permission of *The Scottish Sun*, courtesy of Steve Welsh)

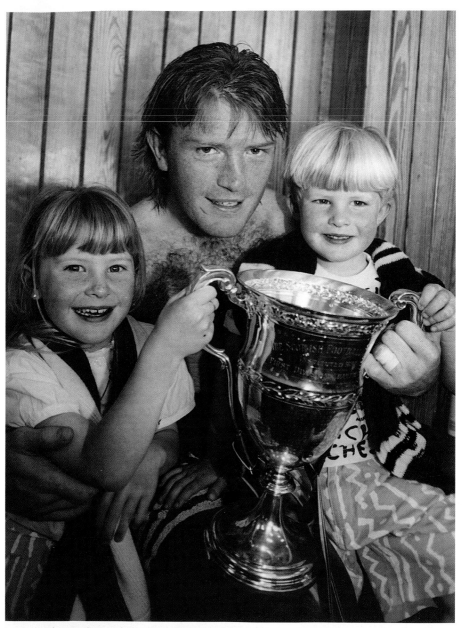

Carly and Lee help me toast a title success (Reproduction by kind permission of *The Scottish Sun*, courtesy of Steve Welsh)

Clarence Seedorf is desperate for my shirt after the Euro 96 clash with Holland (Reproduction by kind permission of *The Scottish Sun*, courtesy of Steve Welsh)

Captain Stuart picks up the man-of-the-match award against Celtic (Reproduction by kind permission of *The Scottish Sun*, courtesy of Steve Welsh)

Meeting the Queen at Bradford City with Sir Bobby Charlton
(Reproduction by kind permission of *The Telegraph & Argus*, Bradford)

Wife Tracey and children Carly, Lee, Craig and Victoria (in age order)

To my pleasure news came back about some of the 'enjoyment' going on among the players. After a couple of pit-stops from the airport to their hotel Durranty had to be put on a baggage trolley and dumped in his room, Goughy needed a wheelchair, Juke Box had christened the foyer with the contents of his afternoon's intake and best of all the model athlete, Brian Laudrup, was found on hands and knees in the corridor at three in the morning by the club doctor and promising as best he could never to touch another drop again. As soon as the troops came back the gaffer came into the treatment room and apologised profusely to the four of us, saying at least he knew what to expect from us. The others were unpredictable. I think that is the only time Brian got blitzed in his days at Rangers. The boys didn't have a game for ten days so there was no harm done and they were returning in good spirits ready to win another title.

I had been carrying an Achilles tendon injury and although I never missed any games I wasn't training and I knew that once the title was won I could head to London for an operation. Unfortunately I got another injury with seven games to go when we played Dundee United. Billy McKinlay caught me with a tackle and I damaged the medial ligaments in my right knee. It was the beginning of a major problem, but I didn't realise that at the time. Because I was going to miss the final games with my knee it was decided that I should go for the Achilles op sooner. My knee, we thought, was just a twist. I didn't know the ligament was torn. The lads won the title with five games to go against Hibs and I managed to make the celebrations on the pitch on my crutches. The Achilles problem was down to wear and tear, something which happens when you play so many games. Rest may have cured it, but I wanted to be playing again as soon as possible and I wanted to be back for the next season. I took a cortisone injection in the knee at the same time and with a break that summer I had no cause for concern.

Chapter 15

The Geordie genius

The news that gave me and everyone else at the club a lift in the summer of 1995 was the controversial signing of Paul Gascoigne. There was a blaze of publicity and talk about the wisdom of the move but he quickly became one of the best-loved players at the club both among the fans and the players. Although it was an inspirational signing it also made my job much more difficult, and the challenge was no bad thing. With Laudrup also around it meant there were only a couple of midfield places going. I was just as positive when I heard Gazza was coming. It was like Norman Whiteside arriving at Everton. I wanted to be beside him, I was hoping I would get the chance to be the man to get him the ball. There was plenty of competition with the established men and the emergence of young Charlie Miller. The year before had been about the fight for the strikers' jerseys with Gordon Durie joining to add to an already impressive array of forwards. I knew Gazza's coming would gee me up too.

My first impressions of Gazza in training were about how remarkably fit he was. He had been out with injuries and as he explained he had gone through six months of hard work in Italy with Lazio to recover. Like most people I thought he would be overweight and struggling with injuries, but he was slim and in good condition. He was miles ahead of me in the pre-season runs. I was left breathing out of my backside although I did have the excuse that the knee was still not right. There he was 50 yards in front of me and I was supposed to be the engine of the team.

If Gazza had any dreams about a quiet introduction to the Ibrox dressing-room he was sadly mistaken. He was soon destroyed by Durranty, Coisty and Fergie. I had also drawn the short straw and was on the next peg to him to get changed every day. This was a nightmare over the years as he had an annoying habit of coming into training with no socks or belt for his trousers. He was always in a rush, never one for organisation in his life. The number of times I came back from training and found my socks and belt had gone were countless. If I was lucky he stuffed a three-day-old smelly pair in my shoes for consolation. A crazy man at times but brand new, as we say.

I think Gazza's first days at the club were spent with his mouth wide open in amazement at the level of banter and stick being handed out among the lads. There was no resting place for him either and every time he spoke to join in and have a go back Durranty would shoot him down with his favourite line in reply to that Geordie accent: 'Get the marbles out your mouth.' He just could not get a word in edgeways, but he was settling in and you could see he was enjoying the atmosphere on and off the park. I think after being in Italy for so long he just loved the voices and also the attitude. There were no superstars allowed at Ibrox – the Rangers dressing-room has never tolerated that. On the park, though, he was the man. If Laudrup had been king the season before Gazza took the throne straightaway.

The season started with a tough European qualifier against Anorthosis from Cyprus. It was early on for us again and we scraped the home leg 1–0 when I put Jukie in for the only goal. We gave a battling performance over there and made the Champions League group stages. The league season kicked off with a 1–0 winner against Kilmarnock with me popping up for the late winner. After I scored in the Coca-Cola tie against Stirling the lads thought they had found a new goal machine, but needless to say they were wrong.

I was having trouble with my knee and missed the first European match against Steaua in Bucharest. The team was not settled yet – Oleg Salenko arrived off the back of scoring goals for the Russians in the World Cup. Maybe the language barrier didn't help him but he never really mixed and didn't stay long. Big Basile was also causing disruption with his attitude. He was a bad apple with a rebel mentality, doing silly things like turning up for training in jeans and tee-shirts when he knew there was a rule about wearing a shirt and tie. Rangers are the only club with that policy in Britain. That particular rule shocked me when I joined – I think I only had two ties. Most of my signing-on fee was blown on a new wardrobe of clothes. I had just signed a deal with Nike who supplied me with loads of smart training gear and I couldn't wear it to the club. There are certain traditions that should be maintained and I don't mind the dress rule at all. If it means you have to be smart then fair enough. It also gives you a chance to slaughter your team-mates about their clothes. Durranty is the biggest fashion victim – he is head and shoulders above the rest. Derek McInnes is a smart lad too although Charlie Miller's Al Capone suits may one day come back in.

I was fit enough to face Borussia Dortmund in one of our best performances of the season. We were very unlucky only to draw 2–2, but we showed what we could do and suggested that this side had a bit of potential. Gazza really made his name in the next game, his first Old Firm match when he was brilliant and scored in a 2–0 win. He also found out straightaway what it meant to the punters. He was as charged up for that one as any of the Scottish boys. That was the only defeat Celtic suffered that season. They were a far better rival with Tommy Burns in charge. For a change we had real competition. Burns brought a desire to their side and a commitment that was missing under Liam Brady and Lou Macari. He was a dedicated man and worked hard. I had a lot of time for Tommy – when he was boss at Kilmarnock I would help out when he did coaching sessions at a club near where we lived. I was not the only one who respected him at Rangers, a lot of the players did too.

Our season went horribly wrong with a double disaster against Juventus. We were gubbed 4–1 in Turin. I came off with damaged ribs and was out for a few weeks. We lost the return 4–0, but that slightly flattered them. From being looked on as a team that could challenge in Europe we had become a whipping boy for Juve who did us 8–1 over the two legs. It showed just how far away from the best we really were. We were not good enough, that was the realisation. It was hard to take and made us all look at ourselves. It struck me that our previous success had been down to the fact we had so many players at their peak at one time. Maybe that was as good as it gets. Seeing the likes of Del Piero, Deschamps and that man Sousa again was watching world-class players perform. My record against Sousa is played three, lost three, goal difference of 13–1. I'm glad I don't see him too often. He is probably the best player I have come up against in that position – his awareness, strength, range of passing were wonderful. He had everything at that time when he was at his peak. The difference was in the organisation too. All through the side they had ability, but they were also a team. Their work rate was huge. We couldn't get the ball off them to make an impression and even in Italy I felt they beat us with another gear to come if they needed it. Everyone slated us but we finished the group by drawing with Steaua and holding Borussia in Germany, not bad considering what a good team they were. That was overlooked in the Juve aftermath.

At least we had the league fight for consolation and had a thrilling 3–3 draw with Celtic. This one was going to the wire. Because Celtic drew 11 of their games that probably cost them the title. We also beat them in the Scottish Cup semi and rounded off a good campaign in the championship with Gazza having a memorable one-man supershow against Aberdeen. The celebrations were incredible that day. One of the great things about Rangers is that they let your kids mix in on big occasions like that. One of my happiest pictures is of Carly and Lee on the team shot as we rejoiced at winning our latest title. We had a long night as Gazza was heading into town to collect his Player of the Year award. Fans were mobbing the bus in the street and it took us ages. They enjoyed it because we had beaten Celtic in a tight finish and that was more important to them too. It was the first time I had known that kind of competition and it made the whole scene more interesting.

I think Celtic helped us win the Scottish Cup that year too. We were so sharp at the end of the season from all that high-powered stuff that we simply ripped into Hearts and gave our best display in a final for years. Gordon Durie scored a classic hat-trick while Lauders, the man of the match, got the other two. That did not happen in past years because we had gone slack and were just playing out seasons, but thanks to Celtic's rivalry this time we were still flying and completed the double with a little help from our 'friends'.

I only played in 19 Premier League games that season because of my knee. I could not strike the ball properly. I remember one goal against Motherwell from 20 yards but it left me in agony. There was a picture of me in the paper turning away after the shot with pain etched in my face. The running, twisting and tackling never gave me a problem, so I got by and nobody really noticed my big secret. As long as I kept away from 20-yarders I would be all right. When you speak to people about knee injuries they say it's the twisting and running that's the hard part, so I thought I must be okay. I believed a rest would make it better before Euro 96.

The season whizzed by although I did manage one special fixture of my own when Tracey and I got married in a quiet ceremony in Callander. The boss even gave me an extra day off for my honeymoon. Now that's generous!

Although I didn't play so much I felt I helped Gazza and it was undoubtedly his season. I gave him as much freedom as possible and kept him away from defensive duties. I tried to get him the ball about 30 yards from the opposition's box and let him get on with his magic. He didn't shirk hard work, it was just better that he did the damage in their half. The season was full of great moments on and off the park thanks to him. The lads were socialising to the full at the right times. Gazza got slammed for saying that the boys liked to go out for a drink, but that was only part of the picture. We were very much full of the other kind of spirit and had a togetherness that shone through on the park.

One of the best tales of those days was when the boys arranged to meet up in a pub in the town but Gazza, Durranty and myself stopped off on the way at the wee man's 'local', the District, to drop off tickets. Gazza was mobbed and one old dear, who must have been over 50, hugged him so hard and wouldn't let go. She did a deal that she would let him leave if he swapped his Rangers top for hers, which she was wearing. Fearing for his safety Gazza agreed. Durranty's pal took us into town and on the road we whiffed this awful smell coming from Gazza. It was the woman's top he was wearing. We ordered him out or he couldn't come to the pub with us. In the city centre we pulled up and Gazza jumped out, dashed into a Sue Ryder shop, saying he would be just a minute and that he would be back with a new tee-shirt. Nothing prepared us for the sight of Gazza emerging soon after in a blue-and-white floral dress. Anyone who saw that must have been amazed. And that was him sober! We got to the pub, past amazed people in the street, and Gazza sat down at the table in his dress for a game of dominoes. It was an hour before he sent Jimmy 'Five Bellies' Gardner out with a hundred quid to get him a Versace shirt. The one he came back with was a howler and I thought Gazza looked better in the dress, so he kept it on for another hour.

Gazza was a really generous person too. That day the local paper boy came round with the *Evening Times* and Gazza organised a whip-round for him at a tenner a time. Now the rumour is that when Gazza asked Davie Robertson for his ten the slightly tight Aberdonian produced a ten pence coin. I can categorically deny this . . . it was actually two five pences. Still the kid went out with about £150.10 in his pocket for one sale. Robbo loved his reputation as a miser but took it a bit far once when he was given a club tartan rug for playing in a testimonial. One of his team-mates was shocked to get it as a wedding present from Robbo later. On the park Robbo never short-changed Rangers. He was excellent in defence but also a threat going forward. To sum him up in a nutshell, he was badly missed when he left for Leeds and was very difficult to replace.

The boss, Walter Smith, had a great feel for when to take us out of the limelight, especially with Gazza in our midst, and let us enjoy ourselves. A perfect example was when he arranged a break in London in the second half of the season. After a couple of stops between the airport and the hotel we rolled into the Hard Rock café with the gaffer, Archie and a few of the coaches. Charlie Miller after one too many even asked the waiter for the hotel key, not realising this was a separate restaurant.

Gazza took us to Covent Garden to visit some of his haunts and we stopped off to listen to a busker. He had just a couple of quid in his cap, but was playing his heart out and was brilliant on the clarinet. Gazza gave him £20 for a Beatles number. We just listened to him for ages and his hat was getting full as he played our requests.

The boss and Archie forked out for a version of *When the Gers Go Marching In* and then the gaffer led us on a conga, singing along. There were a few shocked onlookers to say the least. I promised not to tell that one, but now he has gone I'm in the clear. Sorry, Walter. But it was a magnificent night.

Coisty had managed to find eight tickets for the Wales v Scotland rugby match the next day in Cardiff. Durranty, Archie and Davie Dodds got one each, leaving the last four to the boys who got up first in the morning. I fancied that idea, so went home early. I just made it with Gary Bollan, Ian Ferguson and Alan McLaren making the final four too. The rest came down just as we were going. We made the station at nine which was not a great idea as the train was 45 minutes later. We had to follow the assistant manager's orders and head for the nearest pub. There was a great atmosphere on the train and being patriotic I was looking forward to seeing Scotland play an international without being personally involved. Gary and Alan, the two youngest, were sent to the buffet and announced that the train's stock of Murphy's was out. Coisty was devastated and called for a 20-second silence in the carriage. Screaming kids, a man on a mobile phone and a few other rowdies observed it, totally puzzled.

To make the day complete Scotland won a memorable match and only a couple of the lads, Fergie and me, made it back to London to our hotel as the others lapped up the occasion. On the Sunday I treated the boys to lunch as I had not had a proper stag do before my wedding. The Welsh stragglers came in one by one. Coisty could not face alcohol for the first time in living memory. He had been suffering from too many Cardiff cocktails. Wee Charlie was slating him, but without batting an eyelid Coisty replied: 'Just stick to what you're good at drinking, wee man, and finish your soup.' The last one back was Doddsy, still sporting a silly tartan bunnet with ginger hair and with one can in one hand and another in his pocket. 'Some place that Dublin,' he said. He had bumped into two big Scottish lads and gone back to their hotel to crash for the night. He said he woke up shocked with a big backside in his face. 'To be fair the other lads probably got a bigger fright waking up to see Doddsy,' Fergie added.

Gazza was with us on the Friday night but went home to see his wife who was expecting their first child. He was determined to show us a good time in London, but was not deserting his fatherly duties. Sheryl was not due to deliver until the Saturday night or even Sunday. She thought he should be there. I know he made an effort the next day, but they had words and he headed off to Newcastle. He missed the birth. Gazza took some criticism for that. All I would say is that it was not his fault their argument hit the papers. It's strange everything he seemed to do ended up against him in the press. He certainly wasn't being cold-hearted over the birth, just the opposite.

That was a good season for us overall, but was soured by some headlines about the way we went on off the park, like the rugby international. I thought it brought us together and I will always believe that the way the manager came out with us and could be one of the lads was a master stroke rather than a mistake.

Chapter 16

Euro 96

When Craig Brown was named Scotland manager I was delighted as I had always got on well with him and he was usually very supportive. He was the man who gave me my under-21 debut and that was the start of it all for me. Like Andy Roxburgh he took us to America to prepare for the European Championship finals in 1996. The Rangers lads had been celebrating the Cup win just three days before and we also had a big function afterwards. The last thing we needed was a five-hour delay at the airport which left Durie, McCoist, Goram and McCall to carry on their celebrations. The guys with most caps also travelled club class, while the others went first class. The Ibrox boys all took advantage of that little rule. After such a long trip by the time we reached our destination we were not sure if it was New York or New Zealand. We were merry by then. Just before we went to bed Craig Brown pulled us and said: 'Is that it? Have you celebrated enough?' He had a smile on his face. I think he knew we were still on a high but now was the time to get serious.

The next Scotland game was days away, so we had time to sort ourselves out. We were not disruptive in any way, it was all just cheerful stuff. It was funny that back in England their players were being slaughtered for their trip to the Far East when Gazza and a few others were pictured in the 'dentist's chair' pouring drink down their throats. Little did they know what we were doing.

In the build-up I wasn't sure of my place. I saw one interview with Craig where he described his midfield as Paul McStay, Gary McAllister and John Collins, while I was only billed as a 'back-up player' with Billy McKinlay. I wasn't overjoyed with that one. It was the first time I had been classed as that since my debut. If nothing else it gave me a sense of determination to prove that I was still good enough to be in the first team. McStay did not go to America because of an injury and that helped me get in. We lost against America with an untried midfield and then flew to Florida to take on Colombia, the big match on the trip, and although we lost 1–0 it was a very encouraging performance. I was pleased with my own performance although I did let myself go a little at the final whistle because I wanted Carlos Valderrama's strip. I asked the ref near the end how long was left and he said ten seconds, so I just ran from my position to get close to the man with the silly haircut. I just ignored the action – the ball was deep in their half anyway – ran past Stewart McKimmie who was nearest to him and made sure that I was beside Valderrama when the whistle blew. People in the stand must have thought I was at my 'headless chicken' act again, but it was worth it. I joked that he was equally desperate to get mine, so it worked out all round.

We lost both games on the trip, but the togetherness was there again and we managed to do things you couldn't manage at home without being pestered. Craig gave us some leeway. We went out and did some jet-skiing, a bit of golf and general sightseeing. Scotland deserve credit for the way they prepare. They keep you out of harm's way and keep you entertained although the players also behave and make sure we don't get too many bad headlines.

The high point of the trip was visiting Madison Square Garden in New York for a Rod Stewart concert. At the end we were invited up to take a bow on the revolving stage. Coisty and wee Badger McKinlay were in their element, milking the applause as they pretended to play the guitar and shouting at the audience: 'We love you Madison Square, we'll be back.'

I was confident I would start the finals in the team, a big day altogether as it was my 32nd birthday when we met Holland. It was a repeat of the Euro 92 opener, but this time we got the breaks. The noise and colour at Villa Park was quite spectacular – it really made the game. We were stuffy and worked so hard, but we needed a John Collins 'hand of God' to go unnoticed when he quite clearly handled to give us a goalless draw. Mind you, it was just one hand. I did a man-to-man job on Clarence Seedorf and thought I kept him quiet although he did have a couple of half-chances. We had to start with a good result as the next one was the big match with England at Wembley, who opened with a draw against Switzerland that was not too warmly received. The media were on their backs after the problems they had on their tour before the finals. Basically we could have buried them on their own patch with a win.

We went down to London on the Friday and visited Wembley to get a feel of the place. It was such a big match, the first time I had met them at full international level because the old, regular fixture had been scrapped. It had meant so much to me as a fan, but I was denied the opportunity of playing in the match with the Auld Enemy because it was rated too much of a risk to arrange. We were underdogs and if you looked at the England team you knew why. For all their problems they had real talent in people like Gazza and Steve McManaman. They had a matchwinner in Alan Shearer. There was experience in Paul Ince and Teddy Sheringham, Stuart Pearce and Tony Adams. They had kids like Jamie Redknapp and Gary Neville, not to mention the second best keeper in the competition, Dave Seaman.

A lot was made of my clash with Gazza. It was one both of us were relishing. We had not spoken since the title celebrations, there was no need to. My last sight of him had been in a blue tartan suit when he was picking up his Player of the Year award. Hopefully he would be in the same condition. There was also a big fuss in our camp about who would get his shirt. Coisty spoke to the man before the game and got him to promise to swap at the end, but Darren Jackson had done the same as he knew him from their days at Newcastle United. I wanted it too, but didn't say although young Carly had been begging me to get it for her. I told that story on a TV interview the night before the match and said how Carly had wanted England to win, but changed her mind to hoping for a 3–3 draw with her dad and Gazza scoring hat-tricks. She always had a good imagination.

We were quite confident of getting a result. Craig brought in John Spencer, my room-mate, because he thought his nippiness would trouble big Adams. He had done well against him for Chelsea in the Premier League. I knew Spenny from our time at Rangers and he was a bubbly little character, a joker then and still today. Sadly it didn't work out for him that day although he did run his wee legs into the Wembley turf. The first half went better than we could have imagined. England seemed nervous and tentative. We definitely had the upper hand, but neither side had a real chance. We were giving our big support cause for optimism – there were 7,000 supposed to be there but looked and sounded like more. Just as we were were heading back to the dressing-rooms at half-time I heard the clattering of studs behind me. I looked round and there was Gazza peeling off his shirt and stuffing it in my hand. 'That's for your wee girl,' he said. Unknown to me he had seen the interview on the telly and remembered. It was an amazing gesture as he had just come off the back of a pretty quiet 45 minutes when you would have thought he would have other things than changing shirts on his mind. It sums up his kindness. I hid it in my bag at the break and didn't say a word. It wasn't the type of thing to bring up.

As we were coming out for the second half we got a shout that England had made a change. Someone said they were putting the number 15 on for Pearce. There was panic as no one knew who the 15 was and the immediate thought was it was Steve Stone, their up-and-down right winger. There was even a thought that it could be Sol Campbell, a defender for a defender. But it turned out to be Redknapp, another central midfielder. There was confusion and for 25 minutes England dominated the match, their only spell on top in the game. Redknapp's introduction helped them, but the more significant thing was an inspired spell from McManaman. I had feared he would be their matchwinner and that's how it worked out. We were slightly disorganised for a few minutes and that's when we went behind. Shearer stole in to head them in front. Goram had to make a blinding save from Sheringham before Seaman did the same from Juke Box. We regrouped and I thought we were taking control, especially when I cut the ball back for Jukie to be brought down in the box by Adams. It was a certain penalty. I was sure Gary Mac would score. There was no argument, he was the spot kicker even though Coisty was on the park. To this day I don't think he struck a bad penalty that afternoon. A bad penalty misses the goal. Gary hit the target and had power in the shot, the unlucky part is that Seaman readjusted and got an elbow to the ball to send it over the bar. I think we were all shocked. Even before we had time to say anything to each other or Gary they were heading off down the park to score the second, Gazza did something that he is always capable of and produced a special moment to score the goal that finished us. I saw him running behind and tried to signal, but he went into the space, lobbed Colin Hendry and crashed in the ball as it dropped. It was a great piece of skill, but if that penalty went in I don't think he would have scored because he was apparently going off the park. There were moves on the England bench to replace him, but in a flash be had shown the difference between a good player and a world-class player.

It was a very warm day and at the end I felt worse than I ever have. It was hard to take and the dressing-room was in shock – Craig felt the same but tried to lift the lads and told us we had done Scotland proud, were unlucky and we could still make it by beating Switzerland. It went in one ear and out the other. We were so mentally and physically fired up after giving so much for nothing. We were not given a chance and yet if the penalty went in the least we were heading for was a draw, we were so close to a piece of history. There were so many individual battles out there that it meant so much to us – Shearer scored against Hendry, Gazza against me. Looking back it was a fair performance, but it didn't feel that way at the time. At full-time Gazza swapped his shirt with Coisty and I wound him up that I would never have taken the shirt he had scored in off him.

We went back to our base in the Midlands. The talk on the bus was about what could have been. Gary was low and kind words were really useless. The lads in the squad tried to cheer us up. Billy McKinlay and Darren Jackson were great, telling us how well we had done. We went for our meal. Gary showed tremendous courage by facing the cameras while the rest of us went to a private lounge in the hotel. With the permission of the management we had a few beers. Colin Hendry, Colin Calderwood and myself slipped upstairs to watch the game on the box again. We must have been some sort of masochists. The game went how we felt it had – we had been in control for long spells but just had no killer touch or final ball. I was furious with the commentator Brian Moore who said it wasn't a penalty. How could he say that when Adams had got the man and did not touch the ball? Yet he insisted he had a bit of the ball. It was what we had come to expect of English bias.

There was a very emotional feel about the night. We went back down to the lounge and the full squad were there. By then they were relaxed and had unwound a little. Gary came back from his TV stint and as he walked in we rose to a man and applauded him, singing his name. That was soon followed by *Bonnie Scotland* from Tosh McKinlay and then all the other anthems in a boisterous hour or so. Jimmy Hill even got a mention. Craig also joined in and there was a tremendous sense of togetherness even in defeat.

It was the ultimate drowning of sorrows. It said something about us that the lads who had not played, who must have been sick at missing out, sat together with the team belting out the tunes. Billy McKinlay and Darren Jackson took it on themselves to cheer me up personally. They were filling me with white wines with soda and revving me up for a song. We retired to bed in the early hours, quite merry but with a sense of determination for the next game.

The next day was awful and not just because of the hangover I had. It was Father's Day but Tracey could not make it down with Carly and Lee as she had been to the first game and was eight months pregnant. The other lads were there with their kids and I just felt out of it. Mine couldn't be there to give me a smile and I just felt so down. I was also low because I worried about my place in the team, just thinking that we would have to beat Switzerland by two goals so that would mean a more attacking team and I would probably be left out. It was getting me in a real state, everything was mounting up and it was a bad, bad day. I didn't go to training because I was in such a bad way mentally and maybe physically. It would only have been a light jog anyway but I couldn't face it. The weather was scorching and I was in a daze.

I thought I had done well enough in the first two games, but I had it in my head that because my goalscoring record was about the level of Jim Leighton's and Andy Goram's the boss would drop me. Later that night I bumped into Craig in the corridor and asked him if I would be playing. It's not normally something I would do, that's not me at all, but I just had to be put out of this self-inflicted agony. Without committing himself Craig looked at me and said: 'Get to bed, get some rest because you'll need it.' I took that as a yes and slept like a baby that night.

Because the Swiss game was on the Tuesday we did not have much time to brood. We were focusing on that game and the task ahead. England was one of the hardest defeats to take, but we had a big match coming up quick. Training was bright and we were so determined to get it right and give the fans a reward for their loyalty. It was the same midfield, so my fears were groundless, but Coisty came in up front to join Juke Box.

Scotland started that game as well as any I can recall, with a blitz in the first 15 minutes. Coisty had two great chances, one that brought out a wonder save and another he should have done better with. We were well on top and then Villa Park, packed with our fans, erupted in the 36th minute when

Ally hit one of the best goals of his career. The boys sprinted to the dressing-room at half-time, really pumped up. We were still on top in the second half, but the Swiss were dangerous on the break and Andy made a great save in the top corner. Everything he had to do in those finals was a test and he passed every one. By now the news was coming through that England were beating Holland 3–0, so Colin Hendry was pushed up front looking for another to get us through. It went 4–0 for England and the big man went back. The shout was to keep it tight as that would have meant we qualified for the second stage for the first time ever. Then we heard it was 4–1, but I couldn't say how long was left and Colin was back up front again. We bombarded their goal but it was the same old story. You lose all track of time, but I do remember there were no more roars so I took it that England were still 4–1 up and we had to get that second goal or we were out.

At the final whistle the realisation sunk in that we had failed and most of the players were in tears. The ovation we got was special, a thank you for our efforts. We were proud of the fans as we always are, but they were proud of us and what we had given them. We were out but you would have thought we had won the championship. As the competition went on each game got better for us – the colour of the Holland game – the vital backing at Wembley and now this Swiss reaction topped the lot. I vaguely remember Gordon Strachan coming into the dressing-room at the end saying he had never seen such a Scotland performance. Those were good words from a giant of a player. He was bursting with pride as well as disappointment. There was nothing to be ashamed of, everyone had been outstanding.

People say that was my best game for Scotland, but while you are out there you can't tell. I've had some good ones in the bigger matches that I am proud of. I just know the desire that night and the pride of playing, among all the lads, was as big as I have felt. We were all drained when we got back to the hotel, but we were proud to be Scottish, not just as players but as supporters. The team had done everything and the Tartan Army had been the best.

From a tournament where I wasn't sure if I was playing it ended as a personal triumph, so satisfying in so many ways. It was heart-warming to come back to Glasgow and for weeks after be greeted in the street by people who wanted to shake your hand. It was humbling to know we had done well for the folk back home. I knew before Euro 96 started that at 32 these could be my last finals, but after playing I thought I had two years left at the top and the next stop was the World Cup in 1998. Or so I thought.

Chapter 17

A painful road to nine-in-a-row

The season began well for me with the birth of my son Craig. Tracey was due on 12 July, funnily enough, but the wee man arrived a week later on the Friday before a pre-season friendly with Clyde. I turned up for the game and arrived in the dressing-room about ten minutes late. Some of the lads had already heard about the birth and one or two asked me what I called him. I said I had named my son after the gaffer. Durranty said: 'Walter?' He looked round in surprise and I said: 'No, Craig, the national manager.' The dressing-room erupted. The boss put me on the bench after that.

Only days later we set off on our pre-season tour to Denmark which left Tracey at home with her hands full. But thanks to her family and in particular her mum Margie she coped with the first few weeks of parenthood. That help has carried on down the years and has been invaluable.

It was while we were over there that Walter Smith gave me the bombshell news that Leeds United wanted to buy me. The way he told me was an even bigger shock. We were walking from the hotel to the training ground when Walter pulled me aside and said Howard Wilkinson had been trying to sign me. Although my agent had heard the same news it had not really interested me. Walter surprisingly explained that with Sky forking out millions in England, I could make far more down there at Leeds than they could offer at Rangers. He knew I had been brought up in Leeds and thought it might be appealing to go back. He thought it was only right to inform me of their interest. Basically if I wanted to go then it was up to me to say. I was taken aback by that. I tossed it over for a day but then told the boss that the money didn't matter – I was happy at Rangers and settled at home. There was no way I wanted to leave Rangers. The boss nodded and said: 'Great, that's all I wanted to know.' It was only later when I told the story to Goughie and Coisty that they said the boss had the same conversation and approach with them. The boss had gone to Richard and asked him about Japan and Coisty about America. He wasn't speaking as Rangers manager but as a friend. He realised we had all given great service to Rangers and was willing to help us leave. I was at an age, 32 at the time, when it would have been a major last jackpot for me and he knew there was a chance of getting better money in England. But I must admit I was relieved he had done the same with the other lads, it was just his philosophy and not a subtle way of showing me the door. At first I thought he was trying to get rid of me, but then I realised he was just being honest and straight. Just like Richard and Coisty I decided to stay. Fortunately for me the club came up with a new contract later on that season, we agreed and they were good enough to honour it despite a problem that was just about to turn my world on its head.

Once again our season started with a big European match. Rangers had signed Jocky Bjorklund and Jorg Albertz, two more big-money foreigners. Jocky was in the Swedish side and Jorg was skipper of Hamburg. Both had a good pedigree even if they were hardly household names. The qualifying game before the Champions League could not have been more difficult, a home-and-away battle with the Russian champions Alania Vladikavkaz. They were the team no one wanted to draw at that stage. We were a goal down at half-time at Ibrox and they were probably counting the money we were about to miss out on in the lucrative later stages. The second half was a revelation. Gordan Petric, Coisty and Derek McInnes scored in a great turn-around. I was chuffed for Derek, for he was Rangers daft and the night meant a lot to him.

We won our three games back home before heading off for Vladikavkaz, the worst away trip I can ever remember. What a place that was. My first shock was opening the door to the hotel room and seeing this ugly black creature on the floor. I yelped. I thought it was a bat. It was only when the maid was called she told us it was only a big cockroach. We kept the windows shut in our rooms in case anything else crawled in. It was uncomfortable as the weather was hot and we could have done with the fresh air. The boys all struggled to get a good night's sleep and it was far from ideal preparation for such a vital match. No wonder the club made special arrangements on the way over, stopping off in Vienna for a night beforehand. More than one night there could have finished us off.

So nobody could have expected the performance we turned on the next day. To win 7–2 was incredible, but on the back of that sleepless night it was a miracle. It was all down to the start. We were two up after just five minutes and it turned into one of those nights when everything clicked. Although they were the champions Vladikavkaz were not the menacing side we had thought they were. It was a great result but I would still put the Leeds game above that in terms of importance. But it must have sent tremors round Europe, not many sides take ten off the Russian champs. We were drawn in a reasonable section with Grasshoppers Zurich, Auxerre and the dangerous Ajax. That gave us real hope of making the second stage again and having a good run in Europe after a couple of bad seasons.

Instead the qualifiers were a disaster. The 3–0 defeat in Zurich was a shocker. We had our strongest team out and we were playing against a side with a lot of Swiss internationals we had just hammered in Euro 96. I think we were just too over-confident, which was not like us. We thought we just had to turn up and get the points. Most of us thought Grasshoppers were not very good, but instead it was we who fell to bits. That was bad enough and the home defeat by Auxerre was just as much of a nightmare. We lost 2–1, but I missed the game with an injury.

The only consolation was beating Celtic in the league 2–0 with Gazza scoring a great header at the end of a classic breakaway. We beat them every game that season and that was the start of the domination over them that year. It's never been done before. It was also the story of our season and the difference between us and nine-in-a-row and Celtic sacking their manager. The boss told us Celtic would have more possession, passing the ball across and back. They were never going to hurt us. It didn't matter that they had so much of the ball, it was what they did with it. That season they had Di Canio, van Hooijdonk and Cadete, three big players in positions where they had suffered in the past – they had always had the midfield but not much up front. Now they had people who could score goals. Despite the numbers they ran up against lesser sides they didn't do it in the big games against us. It is a hard thing to do as a player, just sitting back and letting them have the ball. But we always made the best of our chances and also had outstanding performances from Andy Goram to back us up.

Nine-in-a-row brought a lot of tension and pressure to the club. I thought the quality of the football suffered as a result. The 'eight' side was superb, a good footballing team with a lot of goals. We were pushed all the way and we responded. Celtic would be close again, but the standards were not so good for my money.

The difference between us and Celtic was that our big players, Goram, Gough, Gazza, Coisty and Laudrup, would rise to it. It was just like all those years before on Merseyside when Liverpool would find something to see off Everton, a little touch of extra-special skill that settled a close game. A lot of the Old Firm games were dominated by Celtic. They probably deserved to win at least some of those games, but then one of our lads would do something out of the ordinary to sicken them time and again. Tommy Burns was sacked with people talking about his tactics, but it was the personnel who won the matches just as much.

Andy Goram was always a star of those shows. He is the best keeper I have ever played with or trained with. He is one of the smallest keepers you will see, and he wears those pads round his knees but the saves he makes are amazing. He comes out on top in one-on-ones because of the way he covers the goal. Even after his operations – and he's never been the most athletic – he just went on defying logic. Andy really gets himself up for those games and pulls out all the stops. There are some similarities between him and Neville Southall, but off the field they were different. Andy played hard and lived hard, but regardless of his much-publicised problems once he was on that park he was a superman. Whatever happened away from football never affected him during games. He had a few run-ins with Walter over the seasons, but the boss knew he could rely on him on match days.

Andy went through huge lows after injuries which made him miss out on a large part of his career. It got to the stage where the boss put him up for sale. I don't know if that was a psychological kick up the backside, but I do think the boss meant it and was serious about letting Andy go. The result was that the keeper bounced back and got himself in great condition again.

The best tribute I can pay to Andy is that he is the one player I have played with down the years who has produced consistent enough form to be described as world class. People have a go at the Scottish league and its quality, but if you are a keeper it doesn't matter what level you are at, the ball still has to be pulled out of the top corner. If that save needed making Andy would do it. You could maybe say that Gazza and Lauders found it easy against the opposition at times, but from a keeper's point of view the standard of the opposition does not matter. If there is one regret Andy will have when he looks back at his days in football it will be that he did not make the money that he should have with his ability. At times when his career and contract terms should have taken off he was either injured or not in the right condition where the club were willing to offer him the cash he was worth.

Behind Andy in those Old Firm games, but not far off in terms of importance, was the skipper Richard Gough. As a captain he leads by example and I lost count of the number of times I would see him with blood on his shirt. He is Richard the Lionheart, an aggressive leader. Richard is also single-minded in everything he does, he sets his standards so high and he keeps himself in great physical shape. I thought he improved as every year went by, he got stronger as we reached seven, eight and then nine. He was getting better all the time and I thought he had found the ideal partner in Alan McLaren. He was a good listener and wanted to learn and should have followed in Richard's footsteps. Off the park Richard was also the guy who would know when the boys were low in spirits and would tell the gaffer to organise a day out. He always had an image as a model pro, but Richard knew when to get the boys together and iron things out over a bite to eat or a beer. Not getting smashed all the time, just getting the troops together.

I was not surprised that Richard gave up his Scotland place. He said what he felt and wasn't worried about being picked after that. He made 61 appearances for Scotland and had no second thoughts about his decision. He was at an age where the demands of club and country were getting too much. It was just the extra wear and tear on his body. However, I know that Richard would have been willing to play again for Scotland if Craig Brown had called. It never happened.

Because of his single-minded attitude I think Richard would only make a good manager at a high level. I don't think he could handle anything less than perfection. That's what he strives for all of the time and he would find anything less difficult to accept. Richard showed that in his own decision to quit and go to America. I tried to get him to reconsider, I thought he still had lots to offer. I thought after equalling nine-in-a-row he would want to give it his all to break the record. But he had made his decision and was focused. I think at the end of the season he had twinges of regret, but he wanted to go out on a high and with good memories. He didn't want people saying he was past it or that his legs were gone. Even when he left Richard was the fittest guy at the club. I don't think he let his form dip at any time in that final season, but being the type of guy he is the decision was made and would not be changed. I think he did feel that nine-in-a-row pressure more than anyone as captain and it got to him slightly.

I would have been happy to have some of that kind of tension, but the Ajax game in Europe put an end to all that. We had to beat them away and then at home to get back into the group. It turned out to be the ultimate nightmare for me and the team. Before the match, and for the first time at Rangers, I had been asked to play as a man-marker on little Dani, their Portuguese star. He played just off the front and my job was to stop him. I had done similar tasks for Scotland and it held no fears for me, although he was obviously a clever player.

Although my knee had been giving me discomfort for some time it wasn't a handicap. I was playing through it, but after two minutes Dani fell on my outstretched leg and landed awkwardly on me. I felt it there and then, a pain I had never previously known. It was as if something had gone, not a snap just a big stretch. In the heat of the game I thought I could run it off and with the blood and adrenaline pumping I thought I was fine.

We actually started the game well with Lauders and Gazza missing acceptable chances. Ajax started to dominate and the first time I left Dani to close down the full-back the ball was crossed and there he was to head home. Shortly after Gazza was sent off for a stupid swipe at Winston Bogarde. We were down to ten men and this disrupted our master plan completely. We had to do something as the de Boer brothers were getting well on top. Ronald was now coming from deep and with Gazza out of the midfield there were not enough people to block his way. He was getting to 25 or 30 yards outside our box unchallenged. Goughie was screaming at me to close him down which I would have done normally. But I was supposed to be man-marking Dani and was reluctant to leave him alone. However, it was more sensible to stop the man in the middle who was peppering our goal with shots and generally running the game. So I left Dani again and sure enough the same thing happens, I'm out of it again and he scores a second goal.

We are down and almost out, heading back for the dressing-room and I'm starting to toil with my knee. I asked the physio for a big pack of ice which I slapped on my knee listening to the boss's team talk. The gaffer was going around reorganising us and trying to get our shape better with the ten minutes he has to sort things out. But after he said his piece Archie Knox verbally abused me right out of the blue. I was amazed. Before the game I thought I could handle Dani, but here was Archie saying that basically it was the first time I had been asked to do a man-marking job and the boy I was looking after had scored two goals. That was it, no more reasoning than that. I started to explain, to be fair with Goughie's support, that they were coming through the middle. I had been told by the captain to go into the middle and he would pick up Dani in the box. Archie then astounded me by saying: 'You're never f****** wrong, are you?' That just sent my head going and I exploded. I picked up the bag of ice and threw it down. It smashed into a thousand pieces. There is no doubt that if I had been able to move better, able to get up quicker, I would have been over to Archie and there would have been an ugly confrontation. The lads were climbing in to stop me and the more experienced ones managed to calm me down. The pain in my knee was throbbing, we were losing and Archie's comments were the final insult which made me crack.

Realistically I should have been coming off and the physio told me quietly that I had to. But with my blood boiling I didn't want it to look as though I was backing down after the argument, taking the easy way out. I wasn't coming off. I didn't want to make the knee an excuse, so I just started the second half. I don't believe I did it any more harm as the damage had already been done anyway. The only highlight of the half was when Durranty scored to silence the Rangers fans who had been mocking us with chants of 'We've scored in Amsterdam, you've not', obviously referring to the

Amsterdam entertainment industry. I was carrying my knee a bit but we had to get something out of the game to salvage some pride. The man-to-man marking job went out of the window too – the real damage had been done both to the team and to me.

Throughout all of this Gazza had locked himself in the toilet. He had stayed out of the arguments. He felt so embarrassed and I think he feared getting a doing off the gaffer. He knew he had let us down so badly. He heard later about the bust-up between Archie and me. Gazza pulled me aside on the team bus and apologised that I had got the blast that was probably due for him. He told me as he heard the bang when I had thrown down the ice pack that he thought it was somebody coming through the toilet door for him. To be fair to him he was really sorry that I had taken the blame for a problem that he had started by getting himself sent off for being foolish. He never even got a mention at half-time, which was another reason why I felt so hard done by. I was getting the roasting he was in for if he had been there.

I didn't realise how bad my knee was at the time or even afterwards. At first I was afraid I would miss about three weeks and the Ajax return game. What was originally thought to be a tear in my medial was diagnosed weeks later in London as an injury I had been carrying for almost 18 months. The Dani tackle was just the final straw. The first x-ray showed minimal damage when I was looked at in Glasgow, but after failing to respond to treatment I headed for Harley Street and that was where the news got worse. The surgeon informed me after closer inspection that the ligament was severely shredded and was basically hanging by a thread. All he could do was stitch it together, hopefully tighten the ligament and I could strengthen the whole area around the knee. I was to rest and rehabilitate for three months and then be fit to play. There was a 70–30 chance, they said, that I could carry on without any further operations.

I had the operation on Thursday around four o'clock and was hoping to come round in time to see the lads on TV playing an Old Firm game that night. When I came round the surgeon was explaining that he had done more work than he had expected, but was still hopeful it would be strong enough for me to continue. I never even considered that my career was under threat. All I was bothered about was shifting him and the nurses away from in front of the TV. They were spelling out the details, but all I wanted to do was watch the game. I was still a bit woozy and could not make out the score on the screen. I panicked and thought Celtic were winning 6–1, but a nurse calmed me down and told me the score – it turned out to be 0–1 to us. I had to apologise to the medical staff later. Apparently I had ordered them out in a mixture of panic and anaesthetics. I asked one of the nurses to bring me a pay phone and I rang the team bus, telling them to pass on my congratulations to Andy who had been brilliant as usual. I also asked them if Peter van Vossen needed an appointment with the hospital's optician after his amazing miss late on. The next day I gave this little Irish nurse some stick about van Hooijdonk fluffing a penalty. She had to point out to me that Gazza had missed a penalty too. I didn't remember that bit.

I was on crutches for a month and in a knee brace for two months. It was the nine-in-a-row season and I was missing it. All I could do was be positive and work hard in the gym. I knew if I could build up my strength that there was a better chance of the knee mending because the muscles around it would be stronger. It was a blow but I said to myself that I had been lucky in my career with injuries. I thought it was just a matter of time before I was back. I still went to games, saw the lads, but it was difficult. I had a nagging doubt about the surgeon's words. He had said it was 70–30. I found out later it was only 50–50 that I would be back without needing more surgery. After all that hard work, running and swimming, I could even block tackle against a wall. But the big test was kicking the ball distances over 20 yards. I had been trying it out in the back garden with the kids, but I was still lacking that confidence. D-day was looming, I would have to do it for real. Everyone was asking how it was going. I was saying 'fine' but at the back of my mind there was a doubt. Turning and twisting was not a problem and if it had been in my left knee

I would probably have got away with it. But it wasn't and the moment of truth came when I kicked my first ball with the right. The pain shot through it exactly like it had felt that night in Amsterdam. I knew straightaway my next stop was America and transplant surgery.

It was obviously a blow, a shattering blow, but I knew it had to be done. Durranty, Stephen Wright, Andy Goram, Brian Reid and Colin Scott had all been to the States and were put on the road to recovery. It was frustrating. I had done nine to four shifts for three months and was back to the start again, but I would not let this stop me from playing. My next target was to get ready for the pre-season. Andy and Stephen Wright had needed to go back for more work on their knees for different things, so I knew it was a long road. But I knew I was being looked after by Dominik Cisto, the man who had overlooked Durranty's operation and who was considered one of the top men in his field.

I didn't talk to anyone about it before I left, I just went and got it done. It was hard getting into a positive state of mind again. But I thought that a brand new ligament would mean I would be guaranteed of playing again no matter how long it took. The flight over with Dr Donald Cruikshank was a great help. We were upgraded to the top of the plane and it was luxury, like a top hotel. The Doc was telling me about all the players who had come through it and he was very reassuring. I felt better as we landed in Los Angeles.

After the operation I got friendly with a lad at the hospital who ran a local football team. We were chatting and I found out his job was finding replacement limbs and ligaments for the hospital. He told me that mine had come from a 17-year-old boy – it was his Achilles tendon they put in my knee. He had picked the strongest one available, bought it from a sports injury bank and had it flown in from another state. If those details were not grisly enough he chipped in that the teenager had committed suicide. He had hung himself after failing to do well in his exams. That depressed me. I didn't really want to know that, but I never got the chance to stop him telling his story.

The Doc told me that the operation had gone well, and that the surgeon in London had done the best job possible stitching up the old ligament. In any other walk of life it would have been good enough, but not for football. In truth it had been so shredded that I was always going to need a new one. I had to wait ten days before I could fly home, some problem about flying so soon after an 'op' in case there was any trouble with the ligament and the blood flow. The doctor also wanted to assess how the operation had gone and set me a programme that was fairly similar to the one I had been on. It was now just about getting stuck in. While I was over there I heard that Scotland had drawn 0–0 with Estonia. I figured that some of them must have been under anaesthetic too. I was only thinking about playing for Rangers again, maybe getting a game in before the end of the season or just possibly playing for Scotland in Belarus that June.

I did all my work again for three months until one morning I woke up with a huge swelling on the inside of my knee. There was no pain whatsoever, but it was the size of an egg and had a build-up of fluid which was spongy and moved about. What it did was stop the blood flowing round my knee and I could not carry on with it like that. I could do my running and was getting through my whole routine, but after a session of skipping I could feel it. I had the fluid drained by the doctor and although it went down quickly I wasn't happy. I was getting discomfort because the fluid had reached round to the back of the knee too. I insisted I went back to America for Dominik Cisto to have another look. The Rangers people, the Doc and the physios, assured me that the swelling was probably down to a reaction to the screws that had been inserted in my knee. Durranty still has some of his – they can stay in and not cause any problems to people, but on the other hand they are only really needed for the first few months. Some people get reactions to the metal and after the exercising I had been doing that was happening to me. So I went back to America on my own, and without Doc Cruikshank's influence I travelled second class. As soon as I arrived Mr Cisto confirmed the problem and the reaction to me. He was delighted to have another look at my knee and his work. He was well pleased with the way the knee had knitted. The removal of the screws would only set me back four to six weeks, I was told. Now the target was to be ready for the start of the next season. Mr Cisto was up about the whole thing and confident that everything was going fine.

I had been working tirelessly and was strictly teetotal for over four months when the boys organised a day out at the Scottish Grand National at Ayr. The season was reaching a tense finish and with the team having a gap in their fixture list Coisty arranged a large stretch limo to pick us up at Ibrox at 9.30 a.m. Both Coisty, who had suffered a broken leg, and wee Durranty, whose own fightback had gone on before, knew the kind of torment I was having. I didn't want to go at first, but they told me that every now and again you need to unwind. It was good to be back among the boys even if it was just on a social level. It's safe to say my personal drought ended that afternoon. Not surprisingly none of the foreign lads were among the dozen or so out that day, which says a lot about the different attitudes there are.

I could sense the stress the players were living under that season. The supporters had great expectations and the history was everywhere. Everything we had done in eight years would be forgotten if the ninth title was not won. Nobody would have remembered the managers or the players involved if it had all gone wrong. These lads didn't want to be the ones who let down the club by not making it a record-equalling nine.

With three games to go and a home game to come against Motherwell it was party time. The celebrations were started and in full swing. But a certain Owen Coyle enjoyed wrecking it for us, scoring twice and postponing the coronation. The boys clinched the title with an unusual Brian Laudrup header up at Tannadice against Dundee United. I was there that night which was a small consolation for being on the fringes for most of the season.

It was fitting that Brian scored the goal. If the year before had been Gazza's this was certainly his. He was outstanding, a player with truly special ability. Brian is a great dribbler but he also has an eye for a pass. I think Brian took more pleasure that season out of setting things up than scoring. Yet he still ended up as the top scorer at the club. I find it hard to compare him to Gazza and impossible to split them as the best player I have played with in my time at the club. His running with the ball is amazing. Even in training you can't get near him. When his head is down and you don't think he can pick out a pass he will drill the ball 50 yards to someone he could not possibly have seen.

Brian had a well-publicised blast at Gazza for his drinking habits and although what he said was correct it didn't really need to be put into print. You could never call them bosom buddies, but there was a respect between them. He saw in Paul a great talent which was sometimes being wasted. But that should have been said between each other rather on the back pages of a newspaper. Gazza was not too happy about that. He was surprised that Brian had gone public. But the pair of them sorted it out before the next season began. Brian apologised for the way it had turned out and Gazza accepted his word for it. Away from the game Brian was a family man, usually off quite sharpish after games. His family loved it in Scotland. Even now I would say his lad looks a great prospect who will definitely make it one day. In years to come he will follow in his dad's footsteps and keep up that Laudrup tradition. I wouldn't mind being his agent when he grows up.

The title season finished with a game at Hearts and although we lost it was a big occasion. They had put in giant screens at Ibrox for the fans to see the match beamed back from Tynecastle. The boys were flown by helicopter to the ground after the game to collect the trophy and parade round the park. I had taken Carly, Lee, Craig and Tracey and the rest of the family to watch the screens and I still managed to get in on the lap of honour at the end. There were 30,000 people in that day in lashing rain. Ajax had been my unlucky 13th game of the season and I had only played in seven in the league. But they were seven good ones as I told the gaffer – we won them all. The boss gave me a medal, which was a surprise but a nice gesture. I never got it until four months later, but I knew the boss well enough to believe he would look after me.

On the Scotland front I had managed just a game and a half. The World Cup campaign started in Austria and I was praised to the heavens by Craig Brown as we held out for a 0–0 draw. I didn't think it was my most memorable game, but if I had any doubts about my future after Euro 96 then they were quickly dismissed. Soon after we went to Latvia and Estonia for a double header. I played against Latvia and only lasted 45 minutes when I picked up a knock. Rangers wanted me back for treatment, but it was difficult to get a flight from there. They were horrified to find out I was sitting on the bench for the Estonia match that never was. I wasn't even fit, but I was put as a sub because we were struggling with injuries and a suspension to Gary McAllister. Because of the bonus structure there was also a financial reason for sitting on the bench to make up the numbers, although I would never have been sent on even if the Estonians had turned up. The game lasted three seconds and the banter was flying around. I told John Collins not to be too downhearted as it had been one of his best games for Scotland.

Chapter 18

The end of an era

I worked through the summer of 1997 and never had a break, although the schedule was nicely interrupted by the arrival of Victoria on 11 June, a day after my own birthday. Although we had planned to have another child pretty soon after Craig it wasn't planned to be quite that soon, but she is a delight all the same.

Everything was buzzing for the start of the next season. We had a handful of new signings like Sergio Porrini, Lorenzo Amorouso, Reno Gattuso and Marco Negri from Italy, Jonas Thern, Staale Stensaas, Tony Vidmar and Antii Niemi. There was a lot of talk about there being no Scots in the side at all. I wouldn't say there was a them-and-us split, but boys like Coisty, Alan McLaren and Andy Goram were determined to prove that wasn't going to be the case. As it turned out a lot of the Scottish boys would be regulars.

We were made favourites for the title before a ball was kicked, but I wasn't quite so sure. My only fear for us was that three of the main figures from the defence would be missing. Davie Robertson had gone to Leeds, Alan McLaren was struggling with injury and Richard Gough had gone off to America. The back line was the part of the side that we built on and that was suddenly gone. People were getting carried away about our chances, but I had that doubt in the back of my mind. It was not going to be easy and with so many new boys from so many different countries it would take time to gel.

I started joining in with the bounce games in pre-season. I felt strong and they had pencilled me in for a game against Davie McPherson's Hearts in a testimonial match. But on the day before, in a full-scale practice match, Reno Gattuso fell on top of me accidentally. I was stretching for the ball and he just landed on me. At that moment I felt as though the knee had gone on me again. That was the first time that I had a serious doubt about my future. I was just five minutes into a practice match and I was struggling. I thought if I can't tackle I won't make it back as a player. For the next couple of days I was very concerned, but with the encouragement of the physio Grant Dowie I was soon okay. He told me I was going to get twinges, something Durranty had also warned me about. The masseur Mark Stoll broke down some adhesions, old scar tissue around the knee, and I soon felt better. I was out for a week for what I thought was a career-threatening injury and was back to normal again. All my fears were unfounded. That was the worst time, even when I went through the injury and had the reaction it was never as bad as that. Even striking the ball 30 or 40 yards I was getting discomfort, but with building the muscle up it was getting stronger and the problem was gone.

My first home reserve game was against Celtic and there was an amazing crowd of 33,000 people there, not just for me I should add. It was a great way to come back in a 1–1 draw. Coming through that, especially with a passionate match like that to play in, was a huge boost to me. I couldn't wait to get back in with the first team, but they were flying at the time and beat Hearts and Dundee United 3–1 and 5–1 in the first couple of games, with Marco scoring seven out of eight. In Europe we rolled over Gotu and were drawn against Gothenburg in the last qualifier before the Champions League. Losing 3–0 there was hugely disappointing after we had dominated the first half. We drew 1–1 at home and were out although as a consolation we went into the UEFA Cup where we met Strasbourg.

Before that match I came back as a late sub in a 1–0 home defeat by Dundee United in the Coca-Cola Cup. Gary McSwegan cracked in a blinding 30-yard volley that saw us off. After four full reserve matches I was ready to start and the boss picked me for the Strasbourg squad. That was on 16 September, so my injury had taken me out for 11 months to the day. It was a surprise to me when the gaffer named me in the side. We gave away a couple of penalties and lost 3–1. I thought the result – and the away goal – was reasonable because we had not performed too well, but the boss had an inquest after the game. It was taking time for the new boys to fit in and we felt like strangers more than Rangers. We needed to pull together but it wasn't happening. Our defence was an Italian, a Swede, an Aussie, a Yugoslav and a Dutchman in goal. They are all different nationalities and languages. Communication on the park was hard. A lot of these lads had just come over and would be a success for the club, but at first it was hard to get them together. The Strasbourg game summed up those problems. We were missing the leadership and organisation of Goughie. I noticed the difference in my first game back. We were looking around for someone to take the lead. It used to be all for one and one for all, even in our bad times, but everyone was looking at each other for leadership.

Gazza was left out for the next two games against St Johnstone and Kilmarnock. It was said to be a groin injury, but the truth was that he was axed. The boss played me, Reno and Jorg Albertz, giving him a run in Gazza's place. It was a kick up the backside for Gazza and to be honest he needed it. He had not been performing well and had missed games at the start with injuries. He wasn't 100 per cent right physically or mentally. For me Paul's most successful time was when Sheryl and the kids were in Scotland. He had responsibilities, like picking the kids up from school and taking them home, and he was happy. He loved the job of being a father. When his wife went down south he had a lot of spare time on his hands and no responsibilities. I think he would prefer to be settled down, but it wasn't to be. He had those things on his mind and the gaffer was right to leave him out, although it was typical of Walter to shield him by saying he was carrying an injury when he wasn't.

The alarm bells were ringing full pelt when we crashed at home to Strasbourg and went out of Europe, losing 2–1 after scoring first. We had gone out of both competitions in Europe in a month. The boss came under severe pressure and the fact that Celtic were making a push just added to that crisis. With that background we went to Hibs, who were top of the league at the time, and it was the cue for my one and only bust-up with the boss.

I had been sidelined from training for a few days with a knock I took in the Strasbourg game. The physio told me to rest and I would be okay for Saturday. I was with the lads in the hotel on the Friday and Juke Box and myself were spelling out to some of the foreign boys how important this game was to us and the manager. We were the ones trying to raise the spirits and get us going. People were on a real downer and with Brian Laudrup injured most of the boys thought I would be captain in his place. But on the Saturday lunchtime came the bombshell news when the boss pulled us into a room and named the team. I was amazed to be left out, along with Gordon Durie, and for the next ten minutes as he went through the tactics I didn't hear or take in a word. I was just shocked. As the boys went out to go for the bus I pulled aside the gaffer and Archie to ask why I wasn't being picked for a game that I was really fired up for. The pressure and criticism around the club was huge, we needed to pull together and fight our way through it. Looking at the team we were all over the shop at the time and I thought I could help get the collectiveness back. I had tears of anger and disappointment welling up in my eyes. The boss said I hadn't trained all week and he wanted people who were 100 per cent fit. I was still stunned and then he asked me if I wanted to be sub. I said 'no' and told him I wanted to be playing. It was a crazy thing to say as he wasn't going to change his mind. As I walked out of the room I pulled this big oak-panelled door behind me and with the help of a bit of wind it slammed shut. The noise was like an earthquake. The building seemed to shudder. I was going down this big dual staircase when Walter came shooting down the other side and we met up on the first floor balcony. He caught me and said if I didn't want to be sub I could go and get my stuff and 'f-off' back to Glasgow. I was now shaking with fear as well as anger as the gaffer looked ready to banjo me. It was the first time in all my years at Ibrox that I had a really serious altercation with the manager. I told him I did want to be involved as it was a crucial game, so I would be sub.

I was on the bench with Gordon and Erik Bo Andersson. In the pre-match warm-up Theo Snelders got a bad gash on his thumb and needed stitches. I thought young Michael Rae, the teenage keeper, would go on the bench instead and I would be the one to be left out after my words with the boss. But the gaffer stuck with the three and Theo went on to do brilliantly. He took some stick at times, but he was outstanding that day and in those circumstances that few knew about. It was a bad first half and we were 2–1 down, so the boss was going to put me on for Gordan Petric, but Porrini complained he had a hamstring so Gordan had to put his boots back on and go out there as well. Within 30 seconds we were 3–1 down and I hadn't even had a kick. But we pulled it round. Gazza scored a cracker, Jorg got one and I took great delight in putting a ball through for Marco Negri to win it 4–3.

Although we won I was a bit upset that I had clashed with the manager and the next Monday looked him up in the gym. He was doing sit-ups at the time and I saw him and asked to have a word. He said I could as long as I didn't shout and bawl at him like I did before. We just laughed. I apologised, he said not to be silly. I must admit if I was a manager and someone slammed a door on me I would have been fuming as well.

Richard Gough came back to the team from America which was a big lift for us all. He also went straight in as captain and that was a help too. Brian Laudrup had been skipper, but he was not a natural leader. He showed us what to do by example but he wasn't so good in terms of vocal encouragement. He was the only choice, mind you, as he was also the only player guaranteed his place in the side. We thrashed Dunfermline

7–0, but our inconsistency caught up with us again when we lost a daft goal against Dundee United as Andy Goram tried to go on a mazy round Robbie Winters,

When it came to the big games we had no problems and November was a big month as we played Celtic twice, home and away. The Ibrox match was as one-sided an Old Firm game as I played in, with Goughie scoring the only goal. A few others were kept out by Jonathon Gould. It looked as though we were back to our best, but it was one of our few convincing performances of the season. We got a point at Aberdeen, which should have been three, before the Parkhead game that I feel cost us the title. We went there, Gazza got sent off and Marco Negri still put us one up. But we lost a goal in injury-time to Alan Stubbs, who really should not have been on the pitch at the time. He had already got a yellow card and then pulled down Marco in front of the dug-outs for an offence that was maybe even a red card in its own right but definitely a yellow. If we had beaten Celtic with ten men at that stage it would have been a severe dent to them, but they got back in through someone who should have been off. It was also hard as Gazza's dismissal was soft. He should not have raised his hands, but you would have thought Morten Wiegborst had been caught by an uppercut from Mike Tyson the way he went down. That disappointed me, but it is what foreign players do. They seem to be brought up to dive and make a meal of things, it's part of the game in their countries. I have said the same thing to Marco. He has been accused of that at times when he has overreacted, but that is their mentality. I used to get annoyed with him and I was proved right. He deserved more penalties that season but because he threw himself about we never got them.

The draw with Celtic was a blow as we were on a roll at the time and I don't think we would have been caught if we had put some daylight between us. If we had beaten them that day I don't think there would have been any coming back for them. The boys in the dressing-room were down afterwards. All you could say is that at least we got the spirit back between us by playing like we did with ten men.

We went to Hearts in December and they were flying at the time. Goughie was out and I was captain in his place and playing at the back in his position. I had been vice-skipper for three years and one regret I have is that while Goughie was away I was out injured and missed out on the chance of leading the boys more. Anyway, we put on a really top performance that day and won 5–2 which for me was our best football of the season. We then beat Dundee United 4–1 and looked to have got it together.

I was being shunted around to play a few roles, which was a back-handed compliment. We had a lot of midfield players and I didn't mind going back to defence – it gives you a different look at the game and puts things in a new perspective. I felt really comfortable with it and it is something I felt I could do when the legs start going in my career. I told Goughie you could play with a cigar back there.

I was looking to get back into midfield for the Old Firm match at Parkhead on 2 January. That was one I wanted to be involved in, where it matters and up against lads like Paul Lambert and Craig Burley. But as luck would have it Jocky Bjorkland pulled out and I had to go to the back with Goughie. It was our poorest performance against Celtic and we went down badly 2–0. It was frustrating to play at the back and see them coming through and dominating that midfield area.

We bounced back with a 2–0 demolition of Aberdeen, but that was before a run started where we gave away comic-cut goals that cost us vital points too often. When you think we lost the title by two points you are spoilt for choice to look back at the matches where we blew so many crucial advantages. We drew at home to Dunfermline when they scored with their only shot on target deep into injury-time. We lost at St Johnstone. There are so many games where you look back and think 'if only'. There were the drawn games with Kilmarnock and Hearts where we gave away howlers. It was becoming a regular occurrence with teams not having to work hard to beat us – we were doing it to ourselves. I don't think we played particularly badly, it was just those silly mistakes that were hurting us.

The Killie game paled into insignificance because of a head injury to my close pal Gordon Durie. It was scary. He was toiling for a while. The big man was unconscious for a long time in the ambulance on the way to hospital and we were all worried for him. I managed to track down his family that night to find out he had recovered and that was a major relief. As I've told him since, it's not as if he had a lot of sense to lose anyway.

I was suspended for the first time in my career and missed the away game at Motherwell, another low spot. I had picked up six bookings and four of them were for the first foul I committed in a game. I thought you were allowed a couple, but I was in a rut of being cautioned like that. Because of the mistakes we had made we were now behind Celtic and the Fir Park defeat was a shocker. The only good thing about it was the return of Coisty, who had been on the bench all season and had to sit and watch Marco scoring all those goals. It was hard for him, but he could not complain as Marco was doing so well. Coisty was close to leaving with plenty of teams keen to take him on loan, but in the end a calf injury stopped him moving when Everton came in and that worked out well for us all. He made the most of his comeback, scoring, hitting the bar and the post too. He waited for his chance, got it and as usual took it. We went on a run of six wins in six games with Coisty carrying on by digging us out of a hole at Dundee in a Cup replay. We lost a daft first goal again but Ally came up with a double to see us home.

The St Johnstone game was to be the last appearance of Paul Gascoigne although I didn't think it would be at the time. Gazza had been linked with Middlesbrough and Crystal Palace and the club were willing to accept the fee and listen to offers. I told him not to even think about leaving. I was going off with Scotland, but he stayed behind rather than go off with England who also had a game. He had an injury and, who knows, if he had been away on international duty the deal might never have happened. It was so close to the transfer deadline that he might have missed it. Gazza told me there was no way he was going, he wanted to stay and help Rangers win the title. He had been through a frustrating season of his own with injury and form and he wasn't anywhere near match fit, but he was going to get his head down and be a part of the run-in. That was genuinely how he felt and I know him well enough to believe it. It was only on the Tuesday when we were away that I heard the news Gazza had gone to Middlesbrough.

Paul always wanted to be loved and made to feel wanted. At the end the gaffer had done to Paul exactly what he did to me, Goughie and Coisty in the past when other teams came in for us. He told him that the final decision was down to him. I told him not to worry as this is what had also happened to us. The boss had just told Paul he wanted him to stay, but the final decision was his. He had changed his mind three times in the final day, he was going, he was staying, he was going. What finally made his mind up was that Middlesbrough told him that they would not be there for him in the summer, they were going for promotion and wanted him there and then. What he wanted to do was win the title for us and then go. He knew that Dick Advocaat was coming to Rangers and that he didn't fancy him as a player. It was made clear to Paul by the chairman that he would probably be off in the summer anyway and the opportunity and the financial deal might not be there then. Regrettably he accepted. Even when he made that decision to join Boro I spoke to him later and he was deeply affected and disappointed that his tremendous success at Rangers had come to an end.

The supporters and media all thought we had thrown the towel in and that was my initial reaction too. Everybody in the dressing-room was very disappointed – the players were as upset as the fans. Everybody wanted him to stay. The boys were amazed and I was one of them. When I spoke to Gazza he said he wasn't totally happy with the decision, he didn't want to go. For the first time in years he had found happiness on the park and truly loved the dressing-room craic and the gaffer. It was a love affair with the club as a whole.

It was a tough decision for the club too. Paul wasn't 100 per cent right and in the run-in we would need people who were firing on all cylinders. Jonas Thern and Jorg Albertz seemed to raise their game and rise to the challenge when he left. Over those final weeks I had differing views about whether it was right to sell Paul. Jorg had been outstanding from Christmas onwards and was our best player of the season, Jonas had struggled on and off and only showed his true form in the last month of the campaign. I just wish Gazza had been there for that last home game against Kilmarnock when we needed someone with that spark to win a match like that. He would have been the ideal man to find that little magic.

Gazza's departure was a major downer for the fans but we lifted them by winning back-to-back games with Celtic. The Cup semi was a tremendous win for us, a disappointing first half followed by two classic goals from Coisty and big Jorg. We did the same at Ibrox in the league to complete a head-to-head record with Celtic of three wins and a draw in five games. It just proves to me that we could get ourselves up for those matches and find that motivation we needed. It was just the silly points against teams like Dunfermline that cost us the championship. For the first time in weeks we were top of the league again even if it was just on goal difference. We had four games left and even with three tough ones away we were back in it.

The Aberdeen defeat was a huge disappointment for me. We had peaked in both the Celtic games and couldn't reach that high again. The sending-off of Amorouso didn't help but we were behind by then. I was subbed which I could accept because we were chasing the win. Aberdeen rise to games like that although I was still shocked to see Eoin Jess say that beating us meant more to him than going to the World Cup. It was an incredible statement.

We beat Hearts and Celtic drew at home to Hibs, but the crunch was Kilmarnock at home. We knew it wouldn't be easy as they were going for Europe, but with all due respect if you can't beat Killie at home you don't deserve to win the league. The way we failed just told the story of the season. I don't know if it was nervous tension but we missed our chances and were then caught at the end with a sucker punch. The best part of the day was the response of the fans. There were about 20,000 staying on at the end and we dragged ourselves out of the dressing-room to say goodbye. It was the last time many of us would play at Ibrox and it felt so bad to go out like that. But the way they wanted to salute us soothed some of the pain. We thought that was the title gone but Celtic drew at Dunfermline to take it to the last day when victory would have finished us off. There was light at the end of the tunnel, but really we knew it was in their hands.

We had a surprise party for the boss on the Sunday night and with Celtic drawing at least it made the night bearable. It was our way of saying thanks to the gaffer for all he had done for us. We had known for some time this was also his final season. I think the gaffer was more relaxed during the season, knowing that the end was coming, but it must have been a hard decision for him all the same. To make that break after so long was tough, but I believe it was made by the lack of success in Europe which he always took so badly. That night with Walter was the first of a few emotional evenings in those last weeks. He thought he was going out for a meal with his wife and friends at a hotel. Instead there were about 100 of us, staff and players, who had managed to keep it secret and surprised him by being there. It was a perfect way to treat the man with respect and honour for what he had done for us.

The only memory I want of the last league game at Dundee United was of the fans. We knew Celtic were winning and it was all over but after the final whistle they waited at least 45 minutes for us and gave us a great reception outside. The buses queued up as we drove out and they applauded us. It was their way of saying thanks and goodbye and very touching. They knew it was the end of an era as well.

Some of us old-timers, Coisty and Durranty included, stopped off that night and reminisced about the good old days. We went over those stories rather than dwell too long on the disappointment we had just suffered.

It was now down to us to lift ourselves for the Cup final against Hearts. We had played them four times in the season and were basically on top of them every time. Even when we drew with them we had Goughie sent off and gave away two silly goals. From a personal point of view I was sweating on my place. I had been struggling with a form of sciatica for the last month and wasn't able to train as fully as I would have liked. It wasn't until the Saturday lunchtime that I knew I was in.

It was one game I was desperate to play in. I knew by then there was a strong possibility this would be my last match for Rangers. The chairman had pulled me and told me Dick Advocaat had said he wanted me to stay for one more year and although I wouldn't be a regular I was someone he was keen to have around. I would be part of the squad, but after a career of playing I didn't think I could handle the idea of not being in the side most Saturdays.

The final got off to the worst possible start with a penalty decision that has since been proved wrong. Steve Fulton was fouled by Ian Ferguson, but replays have shown it was outside the box. Nonetheless it was given and Hearts were one up inside a minute. They must have come into the game with a few worries after the way we had dominated them all season, but suddenly they were ahead. If you look at the possession, the attempts on goal and the corners it was obvious we did have a grip on the game even then, but we lost a second silly goal and that was a real blow to our hopes of coming back. We got one back through Coisty and should have had a penalty of our own, but it was not our day. We have played worse and won matches, but that doesn't count much in a final.

I was distraught about coming off with the score at 2–0 but I thought we had time to get back into it. I understood that we were looking for a goal but it was still a sad way to go. I knew when I made that run to the dug-out that it was my last in a Rangers jersey and I was choked. The final whistle brought it all home. Normally the fans leave in their droves when you lose a final, but our people stayed on and cheered us again. They were a credit. Brian Laudrup came over and thanked me for my help in the last four years and it came home that this really was it, the end of so many great days together. Goughie went about saying the same things to people and it all sank in.

This was the break-up, not just of a team but of a group of friends who had shared so much.

We went back to Ibrox for a party with the staff, wives and families. The boss pulled us all into the dressing-room before we went upstairs to the function. It was a tear-filled end. Most of us were caught up with the emotion as he thanked us for our efforts down the years. Goughie replied on behalf of the lads and somehow managed to keep his tears in check. Maybe he will be back sometime so knew this was not the finish! Coisty and I were crying our eyes out and even when I went up to see my wife later I was unable to control myself. I said a couple of words to her and just broke down again. Coisty and Durranty stayed behind in the dressing-room for one last wander down memory lane, alone with their thoughts and tales.

It was such a one-off night, so many people going, even Doc Cruikshank. So many memories and great times coming to an end at once. I pulled myself together and looked out the gaffer and Archie to say how sorry I was the season had ended with no trophies but soon we were into the good old times. We were all of one mind that we had finished without a prize, but so much had been done in the years before that this was still a special bunch of guys. We had so many glory days, so many great stories to tell for years to come, but above all so many medals to help us remember them by.

I have been lucky to be part of one of the great Rangers spells, at a club with so many great people. I was already talking in the past tense as I felt the time was right to go, a natural break with so many others leaving. Something in my head said that was it at the final whistle that day.

Looking back at the season there are so many reasons for the disappointment. One was the influx of so many foreign players at the same time and the problems that causes starting a new team afresh. The boss was forced to be inconsistent in his selections because of injuries. The two £4 million players, Seb Rozental and Lorenzo Amorouso, hardly got a kick through no fault of their own. The two star players, Gazza and Brian Laudrup, had seasons that did not match their best through injuries and off-the-field problems. In Brian's defence he also had the thought of moving to Chelsea and the whole contract business put him under more pressure, though even he will admit he found it a hard season.

I don't think Rangers will ever have the same kind of spirit again that we had. I was privileged to be part of a set-up that I don't believe will ever be matched again at any club. Gone are the days when players stay for six or seven years at one place. The Bosman rule means you come and go, so the togetherness may not be found again. I was lucky to be part of something like that while it still existed. I was in the right place at the right time. It is a natural break now and other people should come in and make their way and hopefully match that success. I really want them to and I also have faith that the Scottish boys like Barry Ferguson, Charlie Miller and Derek McInnes will be part of it. We need those type of people to be in a mixture of talent from abroad, guys who are not just motivated by money but want to play for Rangers.

In the end we were only two points and a penalty away from the double and it was a sad way to finish, a terrible way to see an era slip away. But when people look back I just hope they see the big picture and not just the last year. I trust they will think well of me and say he gave his lot for his team. I can't think of a better tribute.

Chapter 19

World Cup woe

I wasn't back in the Scotland squad when the boys qualified for the World Cup finals by beating Latvia 2–0 at Parkhead in October. I was there with Carly, who was still an England fan, so she was shocked when the fans started singing 'Italia'. She realised that the Tartan Army were shouting for them because they were playing England that night and she wasn't too happy about that. It was a great night for all Scots and I was as pleased as anyone. My brother-in-law Gary and his pal Darren watched the England game on TV and I was delighted that Gazza helped them to a 0–0 draw and they qualified.

In the early hours of the next Sunday I came into the living-room where I was entertaining a group of friends and was handed the telephone. I thought my mates had phoned my English pal Paul in Edinburgh to offer our 'congratulations' to him. So I started singing *Que Sera Sera* and *Bonnie Scotland* down the phone. They were in stitches and tried to tell me they had phoned Craig Brown's house instead. I looked at the phone book and panicked. I said, 'If this is Craig, just to say well done for qualifying.' Then they said they were only joking. The next day I got a call from the *Sun* asking me why I had been singing on Craig Brown's answering machine, so I had been stitched up after all. I couldn't believe the lads had done that to me. However, it was nothing abusive, just a wee sing-song. I would never have done that if I had known it was Craig's phone.

Anyway I got the call-up for the Scotland squad to play in France for a friendly when Paul Lambert pulled out. It was good to be back among the lads and although I was never going to play it felt good that I was still in their thoughts. I was also encouraged by Craig publicly saying he was glad to have me back. I was in for the Denmark game and again Craig was talking about me and saying it was a case of resitting my driving test. Well, I only got 18 minutes as a sub, so I don't reckon I could even have got as far as a three-point turn with that kind of test. I was also in the squad for the Finland game when I really needed some kind of action to stake my claim. I didn't make the bench, but if I had known I would have asked to appear for the B team the night before. I was thinking of asking for that chance, particularly when Steve Fulton pulled out of the B side, but unknown to me Craig had already told the Celtic lads they wouldn't be in the big team. So when I raised the idea with John Collins he said not to worry as he thought I was sure to get a game in the first team. Instead Billy McKinlay and Scot Gemmill started again for the second game running and, hours before kick-off on the Wednesday, Craig told me I wasn't even a sub. It was hard to take that I was being left out completely. Craig told me not to read too much into it, but I knew then that the chances were I wouldn't make France and the finals. I had not been given any chance to show what I could do and that was a major disappointment.

But worse was to come. I was on the top table for a sportsman's dinner at Parklands, where I am a member. By chance Craig was the after-dinner speaker, so I made sure I caught him to have a few words about the squad. It was just before he named the party and I wanted to put my case. It was just as well that I got that opportunity. The matter was preying on my mind, with people saying I would go but deep down I was feeling the answer would be no. I managed to pull Craig aside on the way to the car park after the 'do' and had a chat with him. I told him I wasn't naïve enough to think I would make the team for the opening match with Brazil or play a leading role in the competition, but that he could count on me if he needed me. I said I wouldn't be like an old pro, going along for the ride with a bad attitude. I wouldn't go in the huff over there if I wasn't selected. I just wanted to put his mind at rest that I would be fully committed and totally behind the cause even if I was not going to be a central figure as I had been in the previous three finals. I certainly didn't want him to think I had a 'been there, done that' attitude or would be in any way disruptive. When I made that plea it was only from a professional viewpoint, I knew what I had to offer and that it might only be for one game or part of one. In fact, even if I didn't kick a ball I would still have wanted to be part of it. Craig always goes on about lads like Colin Hendry and Gary McAllister being patriotic, but no one is more fervent than me.

I was pleased to have the chance to tell him that but his reply left me totally stunned. Craig said he feared that Coisty and I, if we weren't picked, were going to treat the trip like a party. Those were his words. He mentioned it two or three times and I found it hard to take in even then. Craig was obviously referring to what I have already mentioned about the flight to America and the night of the England game. It stunned me completely. I guaranteed Craig that would be the last thing on my mind. To even imply that was a slur on me and Coisty. I have never let myself down like that throughout my career. There is no doubt that when I have been at successful clubs I have celebrated off the park, but only at the correct times. As a pro I could never be reproached for anything like that during my career. His exact words to me were, 'Our biggest fear would be that the likes of yourself and McCoist, if not selected, would turn the trip into a party'. He said 'our' because he was talking about Alex Miller, his assistant, as well as himself. We stayed there for about 30 minutes and on the football side he said he knew he could rely on me and knew I had played several positions for Rangers, so I could be valuable to the squad. But it was this 'party' thing that stuck in my mind.

When he said the word party he never mentioned the word drink, but I think that he had that in mind because of a couple of those incidents. I was upset, if he wasn't going to take me I hoped it would be for football reasons and no other. In the tournaments I've been to with Scotland, and there have been three major ones, the camaraderie and spirit has been great. It has to be with Scotland because that is what gets us by. We don't have any individual ability to compare with the best or any great stars. When you are away for a long time you need that spirit, but that doesn't mean I am saying you need to be bevvied. That night after the England defeat was boisterous, but it brought us together and was positive. We showed that a couple of days later by putting on one of the best performances by a Scotland side ever when we beat Switzerland.

After that talk I had real doubts about being named in the squad, but I kept it quiet. Only Craig really knows the full and final reasons. While I can maybe accept there was a case for me being left out on football grounds I don't see how you can leave out Coisty. I spoke to Ally just after he got the news and he was devastated. I was half-expecting the bad news, he was struck dumb. I have to be honest and say that I sensed my own batteries were a bit low after a long season, but I still felt I could have done a job, even just for part of the game, against Norway in the key match of the qualifying group. I felt that was a British type of game and just the sort I would do best in. Okay, there are players who cover that position, but I believed there was still enough left in me for that one.

All I can say about Craig's final decision is that at least he phoned me at a reasonable time. He had called at 8.30 and my wee boy Craig picked it up, funnily enough. Although he said he would ring me one way or another I knew it would be bad news. He said I had come back from a serious injury which was something I had already said wasn't a problem or an issue. After all, I had played so many games that season. Craig told me he was not naming Coisty either but had not been able to get hold of him. I thanked him for his call as it must have been a difficult one to make. I wished him and the lads well and said my only regret was that I didn't get a chance to show him what I could do after my injury. I said it was a sad way for my Scotland career to end – as an 18-minute sub.

At that point Craig said it wasn't the end and in the future he could see me playing at the back for Scotland as I had done for Rangers and I could come into the reckoning. But I said in all honesty if I could not get into the 22 for France I could not really see myself playing for Scotland and pulling on the jersey again.

I didn't know the squad until the day after, when it was announced, and naturally I was disappointed and surprised to see the selection of Tosh McKinlay, who is a smashing lad but had hardly played for Celtic at all in the season. One of the criticisms aimed at me by Craig was not being picked at times by Rangers. The other major surprise for me was that I felt the squad was short of an extra midfielder. Craig said Colin Calderwood could do that role but I look on him more as defender.

This party thing will be in the background when I look back on the decision. It's a nonsense really. Sure we had a few social gatherings at some of the finals, but it was always done in the interests of helping the boys relax. I can't remember it being a problem. The most disappointing factor for me is that I reassured Craig that this would not be the case, but he still repeated his fear. His mind was made up and it was only by accident I found out what he was thinking.

I just wish I had done better in the last few Rangers games – I know my form dipped and that would have hit my hopes. I still feel you should be judged over the season. But even if there were football reasons for leaving me out Coisty should clearly have gone. I never told him exactly what Craig had said – he was too upset about not being picked. He would have found that comment as hard to take as I did. He would have wanted to be selected on his goals and ability and as far as I am concerned that should have been enough to take him to France. Knowing him as I do he was hugely hurt but he kept his dignity.

There is definitely an argument for having Ally around for

team morale alone. When you are away for long spells you need someone to liven things up at meal times and get-togethers. It helps to have a livewire around. I can only think of Billy McKinlay doing that job in his absence. Although Coisty would only want to be in France on his footballing ability and not because of his banter. It's an old-fashioned idea in some ways and it's something that has gone out of football with so many foreign lads coming in. You can't expect them to chip in with the quick one-liners. But I believe there is a place for characters in the game. I've played with plenty of them and can say they are a major part of a successful set-up.

It is sad to think my Scotland career is over. I've been very fortunate to pull on the Royal Blue on 40 occasions and treasured every minute. I've played in all the last three big competitions, Italia 90, Euro 92 and Euro 96 – the only Scot to have done so – and even managed my only goal in the World Cup against Sweden. I thought my experience and commitment might have given me one last chance to perform for my country but it's not to be. I have absolutely no regrets and wish Scotland all the very best.

Chapter 20

Meeting the Queen flanked by two Bobbies

I have gone back to Bradford many times down the years, playing in Mark Ellis's testimonial and Gavin Oliver's. I even opened a suite at the club named after me, McCall's, which was a tremendous honour. We had a ten-year reunion there in 1995 to commemorate the fire and our promotion. Most of the lads were there – Peter Jackson, Bobby Campbell, even Trevor Cherry and Terry Yorath plus Stafford's wife Lorna. It was a nostalgic night, looking back on some great times and raising money for the burns unit. I also went to see Bradford lose 2–0 at home to Blackpool in the promotion play-offs and never imagined they would win the second leg 3–0 and then win again at Wembley against Notts County to go up. I would have been to that one but Scotland were in America for their Euro 96 warm-up tour. I always get a great welcome and see a lot of familiar faces at Bradford. Although the personnel has changed there are still people like Brian Edwards, Alan Gilliver and folk from the supporters club about. The ground has been built up beyond recognition, but the feel of the place is still there.

There was one very special occasion when I was honoured to be asked back down to meet the Queen who was at the ground to open the new stand. Although they call it the Pulse Stadium it will always be Valley Parade to me. The day started badly because my flight to Leeds-Bradford airport was cancelled, so we were rerouted to East Midlands and then bussed north. My dad picked me up and got me to the ground on time. The biggest day of my life and I'm in a mad rush. I was to meet the Queen, the Duke of Edinburgh and also Sir Bobby Charlton, one of football's biggest legends. As we walked out to the centre circle there was Sir Bobby on one side and Bobby Campbell on the other. Just like me the Queen had been delayed, so we were standing around and talking about football. It was great to talk and listen to Sir Bobby, one of the best players of his era. Bobby Campbell was also chatting away about our great teams and I was in the middle interpreting for him, 'What did he say, what did he say,' asked Sir Bobby.

Sir Bobby had met the Queen a couple of times and told me not to freeze, if you want to say anything just say it. I had that thought in my mind as the moment came. I smiled, politely shook hands and bowed. Then I hit her with a line straight out of Cilla Black's *Blind Date*. I said: 'Its a real pleasure to meet you and you're looking gorgeous.' She smiled and said 'thank you' and walked on. She looked brilliant. She had a red hat and suit and for a woman of her age looked immaculate. Just everything about her. And here was me coming out with a chat-up line. It was great to go back to Rangers and have one up on the boys. We have two pictures of the Queen in our dressing-room, but even Coisty has not met her. He got his MBE from someone else.

The one question I am always asked about Bradford is if I would fancy being manager of City one day. Only last year when Chris Kamara was sacked I got a call asking me if I wanted the job. It wasn't a direct approach but I got the message that if I wanted the job it was mine. I was genuinely flattered, but the timing wasn't right. I still wanted to play for Rangers and had the World Cup in 1998 on the horizon. It just came too soon – it's hard enough playing without managing. I still felt as though I had got enough left in me for two more years without taking on that extra burden. However, it is one thing I would really want to do in the future.

If I ever become a boss I will give it the same qualities I have given in my playing career, to be fair, honest and fully committed. I've been lucky in my career and never played under any bad ones. I do feel the desire to be a manager inside me, but there is no guarantee I would be a success. I thought Terry Butcher had everything to be a top manager one day. He had all the qualities, but sometimes you are only as good as your chairman will let you be. You also have to be fairly lucky and get the right break somewhere. I might have to start at the bottom and coach kids, but that would not be a problem. I could not handle not having football in my life. The year I had out with injury has maybe added another year to my playing career. I used to think at 32 or 33 I might start phasing myself out but that point of view has changed and I believe I have extended that 'retirement' date for a while.

One day in the distant future I would love to manage Bradford. If I had the choice that would be where I would start. I would like to try and repay the Bradford fans for all their support and courage those years ago. There is some unfinished business to be done as far as I am concerned. I have never meant to put pressure on the manager in charge at Bradford at any time, I am talking about down the line. It is a dream and I want to make it a reality. What amazes me is that the club has been in the bottom four of the First Division at times and still pulls crowds of 15,000. It shows the potential of the place – they can pull people in from all over the city. They took 30,000 to Wembley so that is the maximum support you could look to draw in. I would love to think I could do as a manager there what I never quite did as a player and take them to the top flight. It is hard these days with finances – clubs in the English First Division have an uphill struggle – but money does not always guarantee success. We proved that in Trevor Cherry's day. It would be harder to do that now because you are up against so many £1 million players. But I know that success comes mainly from team spirit. I have found that in the triumphs and disappointments I have been through as a player.

I have seen what happened to Walter Smith down the years,

the way the strain has aged him. I have also seen Kevin Keegan and Kenny Dalglish come under pressure. It makes you think if you want that. But how else do you stay in football?

I don't want Rangers supporters thinking I was desperate to leave, far from it. When you have been at a club like Rangers so long it is a massive wrench to leave everyone there, like Peter on the front door, Laura the gaffer's secretary, the kitchen girls, the maintenance staff, the ticket office people and the folk on the commercial side. Especially the great John Greig, who has been a tremendous influence and a good friend. Walking out of that door for the final time will be a nightmare.

Wherever I end up, Rangers will always be in my heart. I've spent an unbelievably happy and successful seven years there and no one can take away my special memories. I will definitely be back to watch the boys and, as the saying goes, 'You'll never be a stranger once you've been a Ranger!'

Chapter 21

Thanks for the memories

At this stage of most football books you normally name your best all-time team. In all honesty, because of the number and variety of guys I have played with over the years, that is an impossible task. For example just start with the goalkeepers. Jim Leighton over the past few years for Scotland produced countless outstanding performances and got us to Euro 96. Neville Southall was at his peak when I was at Everton, not just in games but in training. I never thought I would see a better one, but as I have already said Andy Goram is for me simply the best. He is the one real world-class player I have played with.

Throughout my career I have played with some great club men, Dave Evans and Peter Jackson at Bradford, Graeme Sharp and Dave Watson at Everton, Trevor Steven at Everton and Rangers, Richard Gough, Gary Stevens and Mark Hateley at Rangers, Tommy Boyd for Scotland. How do you put them all in a team? But how could you have a team without them?

There are those whom you would want in the trenches, the 100 per centers, Greg Abbott at Bradford, Peter Reid at Everton, John Brown and Ian Ferguson at Rangers plus big Colin Hendry for Scotland. You need these lads who give you everything to be in your side.

Then there are the people with tremendous ability,

Bradford's John Hendrie, Everton's Norman Whiteside and Pat Nevin who have genuine skill. How do you leave out Brian Laudrup and Gazza or Gary McAllister and John Collins from Scotland?

You also need characters in your dressing-room, guys like Bobby Campbell and Ces Podd at Bradford, the crazy Peter Beagrie at Everton and the dynamic duo of Coisty and Ian Durrant at Rangers. Scotland have Billy McKinlay and John Spencer to liven them up.

Finally, I would want some of my room-mates in there, Mark Ellis and Don Goodman at Bradford, Neil McDonald and Tony Cottee at Everton, Disco Dale Gordon and Gordon Durie at Rangers and Scotland.

As you can see from the names and various qualities it would be impossible to fit them all into a team, but they have all given me great times and memories.

When it comes to managers there has been George Mulhall at Bradford along with Brian Edwards and Lammie Robertson who gave me great encouragement. In my early years, in Roy McFarland and Trevor Cherry I had two men whom I learned from, while assistants Mick Jones and Terry Yorath passed on their knowledge and reading of football. Terry Dolan got my respect for his training and tactics with an excellent number two in Stan Ternent. I enjoyed my time under Colin Harvey and Howard Kendall had his interesting and successful management style.

Finally there was Walter Smith. Although I never saw much of his coaching, which he did under Graeme Souness, the respect he has from everybody is incredible. From players to managers to the media I have never heard anyone have a bad word to say about him. I never knew him before I joined Rangers, but it was through talking to people like John Collins and Pat Nevin, who had worked with him before, that I got a picture of what the man was like. All the compliments have certainly proved correct. I think it all comes back to his honesty. He has got a great desire and strength of mind to succeed. Of all the bosses I have played for he is the one I would least like to cross. The mixing off the field was as big a part as what happened on it, the camaraderie he brought along with Archie Knox's help was what made the club so successful and a happy place to be. One story that sums up the way he bonds people and has his own special touches comes from one night before a Scottish Cup tie at Motherwell. He gathered us together and brought out the Cup itself. He got us to toast the trophy and we went out and won the next day. We would go to hotels on Hogmanay, usually before the Celtic games, and he would invite us to his suite to bring in the New Year. He made sure all the staff and the players were there and then we were back to bed. It was little touches like that which put him apart.

The boss was inspirational. Very rarely did he lose his temper. But you were left in no doubt when he did what he wanted from you. His door was always open. If there was a problem he was never a believer in fining people. Over the years he has had to deal with some larger-than-life characters. He has got everyone's respect for the way he has handled those difficult situations. Any time he had to say something harsh to a player he never did it in public. It was always behind closed doors. Sometimes we deserved it, especially after some inept European performances, but he would shield his players from the blame and take his share on the chin. The only criticism levelled at him is his transfer record. Some of them have not paid off, especially a few of the foreign ones. However, those like Laudrup, Gazza and Albertz show that he is no mug in the market. He was also lucky to have the enthusiasm of Archie Knox and coaches like Davie Dodds who were great buffers between players and management. The one thing I would like to take from the gaffer into management myself is his calm, quiet, non-celebratory manner when we won something. At the end of the night he would always manage to get up on the table and belt out a Bon Jovi number or *Simply the Best*. He more than anyone has been the biggest influence in my career.

On the international front I enjoyed my time both under Andy Roxburgh and Craig Brown. Craig, like Andy, was very passionate, thorough and meticulous in his planning. He also encouraged input from the players although the final decision was obviously his. He gave me my first cap for Scotland with the under-21s and my last and 40th against Denmark. And even though he never selected me for the World Cup, I hold no grudges and wish him well in the future.

I have also been fortunate to have great fans on my side. The loyalty and courage of the people of Bradford, the patience of the Everton support, especially after my first season, and of course the huge and fanatical following of the Teddy Bears. The Tartan Army will hopefully forgive me for my early aberration in picking England first and I hope they appreciate me as much as I appreciate them for their backing around the world.

I have had a limited amount of ability, a strong engine and a good attitude to make a living out of the game. I have played with and against great players for good, honest men and managers in front of loyal and passionate supporters. I've given my best and thoroughly enjoyed the successes along the way, with many magic moments to treasure on and off the park. Hopefully I have made good friends and not too many enemies. I still have strong ambitions and dreams to fulfil and if the next 30 years are as much fun as the last I will be delighted.

But it's been off the park where I have been luckiest of all. I have had two loving parents and a supportive family, four wonderful kids in Carly, Lee, Craig and Victoria, a super wife in Tracey and her family, many close pals and too many memories to mention.

I hope you have enjoyed reading the book as much as I have enjoyed writing it. I was going to call it *Dreams Come True*, because if you believe that in your own life it can happen – and I'm the proof. Give it your best shot and be lucky.

Appendix

Stuart McCall
career statistics

Bradford City

1982–83   Debut v. Reading (28.8.82); 25 League (plus 3 sub) appearances, 4 goals; 2 FA Cup appearances; 2 Milk Cup appearances

1983–84   46 League appearances, 5 goals; 2 FA Cup appearances; 4 Milk Cup appearances

1984–85   46 League appearances, 8 goals; 3 FA Cup appearances, 1 goal; 4 Milk Cup appearances

1985–86   38 League games, 4 goals; 4 Milk Cup appearances, 2 goals

1986–87   36 League appearances, 7 goals; 3 FA Cup appearances, 1 goal; 1 Littlewoods Cup appearance

1987–88   44 League games, 9 goals; 2 play-off appearances, 1 goal; 3 FA Cup appearances, 1 goal; 6 Littlewoods Cup appearances, 1 goal

Total   **267 (plus 3 sub) appearances, 44 goals**

Everton

1988–89	29 League (plus 4 sub) appearances; 4 FA Cup (plus 1 sub) appearances, 3 goals; 4 League Cup appearances, 1 goal
1989–90	37 League appearances, 3 goals; 7 FA Cup appearances; 4 League Cup appearances
1990–91	33 League appearances, 3 goals; 5 FA Cup (plus 1 sub) appearances; 3 League Cup appearances
Total	**126 (plus 6 sub) appearances, 10 goals**

Rangers

1991–92	35 League (plus 1 sub) appearances, 1 goal; 4 Skol Cup appearances; 3 Scottish Cup appearances; 2 European Cup appearances, 2 goals
1992–93	35 League (plus 1 sub) appearances, 5 goals; 4 Skol Cup appearances, 1 goal; 5 Scottish Cup appearances; 9 European Cup appearances
1993–94	34 League appearances, 3 goals; 2 League Cup appearances; 6 Scottish Cup appearances; 2 European Cup appearances
1994–95	30 League appearances, 3 goals; 2 League Cup appearances, 1 goal; 2 Scottish Cup appearances; 2 European Cup appearances
1995–96	19 League (plus 2 sub) appearances, 3 goals; 1 League Cup appearance, 1 goal; 4 Scottish Cup appearances; 7 European Cup appearances

1996–97	7 League appearances; 2 League Cup appearances; 4 European Cup appearances
1997–98	26 League (plus 3 sub) appearances; 2 European appearances; 1 sub appearance Coca-Cola Cup; 5 Scottish Cup (plus 2 sub) appearances
Total	**254 (plus 10 sub) appearances, 20 goals**

Scotland

1989–90	8 caps, 1 goal
1990–91	3 caps
1991–92	9 caps
1992–93	3 caps
1993–94	4 caps
1994–95	3 caps
1995–96	7 caps
1996–97	2 caps
1997–98	1 cap
Total	**40 caps, 1 goal**

Honours

Bradford City	Third Division champions 1984–85
Everton	FA Cup runners-up 1988–89
Rangers	Scottish Premier League champions (6 times) 1991–97, Scottish Cup winners (3 times) 1991–92, 1992–93, 1995–96, runners-up (2 times) 1993–94, 1997–98, League Cup (2 times) 1992–93, 1993–94